Eric Haseltin
Chris Gilbert

RIDING THE MONSTER

FIVE WAYS TO INNOVATE INSIDE BUREAUCRACIES

DISCOVERY DEMOCRACY PRESS

Books by Eric Haseltine, PhD

Long Fuse, Big Bang (Hachette, 2010)
Brain Safari (Greenleaf, 2018)
The Spy in Moscow Station (St Martins, 2019)

Books by Chris Gilbert, MD, PhD

The French Stethoscope (iUniverse, 2010)
Dr Chris's A, B, C's of Health (iUniverse, 2010)
The Listening Cure (Selectbooks, 2017)

Riding the Monster
Five ways to innovate inside bureaucracies

Eric Haseltine, PhD, and Chris Gilbert, MD, PhD

Discovery Democracy, Rancho Palos Verdes,
California, USA

Published 2021

ISBN 978-0-9981228-0-9 (paperback)
ISBN 978-0-9981228-2-3 (epub)
ISBN 978-0-9981228-1-6 (audiobook)

Table of Contents

Abbreviations

ACE	Aggregative Contingent Estimation
AITA	Advanced Intelligence Technology Association
AR	augmented reality
ARL	Army Research Labs
ARPA	Advanced Research Projects Agency
ARPANET	Advanced Research Projects Agency Network
BBN	Bolt Beranek and Newman
BOM	bill of material
CAGR	compound annual growth rate
CES	Consumer Electronics Show
CONOPS	concept of operations
DARPA	Defense Advanced Research Projects Agency
DIA	Defense Intelligence Agency
DOD	Department of Defense
EOD	Explosive Ordinance Disposal
HAC	House Appropriations Committee
HPSCI	House Permanent Select Committee on Intelligence

IARPA	Intelligence Advanced Research Projects Activity
IED	improvised explosive device
IETF	Internet Engineering Task Force
IMP	Interface Message Processor
IOT	Internet of Things
MBA	Master of Business Administration
NCOs	Non Commissioned Officers
ODNI	Office of the Director of National Intelligence
PIPS	Potomac Institute for Policy Studies
RFP	Request for Proposal
RFC	Request for Comment
SSCI	Senate Select Committee on Intelligence
SRI	Stanford Research Institute
UCF	University of Central Florida
UCLA	University of California, LA
UCSB	University of California, Santa Barbara
USTLC	United States Technology Leadership Council
VR	virtual reality

Introduction

Well organized bureaucracies famously chew up innovations — if not innovators themselves — like monsters who roam their domains, sniffing out change-agents in order to devour them. Monster bureaucracies eat both innovators and innovations for breakfast ... and lunch and dinner.

This book will help innovators who work in established organizations avoid being eaten up by the conservative organizations in which they work. More, this book will illustrate how to work around bureaucracy and red tape to get innovations into the hands of customers who will benefit from the innovations, whether those customers are consumers, businesses, government workers, or soldiers.

Innovating inside existing organizations — versus start-ups or small companies — is so difficult because the very name "organization" implies order, rigor, and structure, all of which are explicitly designed to prevent deviations from tried-and-true policies, practices, processes, and products.

And another name for deviations from the tried and true is ... innovation.

By saying this, we do not mean that monster bureaucracies are inherently bad creatures that innovators should flee in their sacred quest to innovate, nor do we suggest that innovators attempt to slay such monsters, because monsters have many positive qualities.

Monsters are good at knowing their customers, and at making, selling, and supporting things for those customers. Monsters have trusted brands, and monsters are good at protecting their turf from competitors.

That's why we advocate riding monsters, steering these massive, powerful beasts in constructive new directions.

In other words, innovate by harnessing monsters rather than fighting them.

This book tells the story of five innovators who harnessed and directed, rather than combated or fled, the bureaucracy of large organizations.

The five strategies we will highlight for steering monsters in new directions are:

1. Give the monster all the credit

2. Don't wait for the monster

3. Harness full monster power

4. Cultivate the right monsters (before jumping on their backs)

5. Persuade the monster to do more of what it does best

This book is also for those of you who are leaders who identify more with the bureaucracy than with the disruptors seeking to shake things up, but who nevertheless agree that change can be beneficial and even sometimes necessary to the long-term survival of the enterprise.

If you're in that category, the book won't so much suggest what to do, but what not to do. The five case studies will show the kinds of behavior towards which you should turn a blind eye, allowing innovators to sneak around in the monster's blind spots for the monster's own long-term good.

Although doing nothing is an anathema to action-oriented leaders, we advocate a strategy of inaction versus action for two reasons:

1. Most attempts to stimulate innovation inside bureaucracies — such as anointing an innovation executive, creating an innovation group, or laying out practices for funding innovative ideas from inception to product delivery — are expensive and produce meager results because formal practices and policies are no substitute for the highly informal, highly personal processes of creativity and its close cousin, innovation.

2. Innovation is, at its very heart, a natural, highly informal social process, whereby the spark of an idea in one person catches fire in a group of

people close to that person. Inside bureaucracies, such groups, forged with bonds of mutual respect and trust, almost always consider themselves to be "a rebel alliance," an "underground," a "counter-culture," or some other form of "out-group." And, strange as it may seem, the feeling of alienation from the bureaucracy these groups often have can be very healthy, because it engenders closeness and a sense of noble common cause that makes the group far more cohesive and effective.

Taking these two points together, we argue that leaders who want innovation to thrive should avoid unnatural, formal processes and embrace more natural, informal processes. Formal processes aim to prevent problems that arise when you just let people do whatever they naturally want to do. As such, they are a reaction to many historical missteps in the organization, evolving into a very long list, saying, essentially, "Don't do this and don't do that."

But creativity and innovation, along with formation of strong emotional bonds among innovative outgroups, are very healthy, natural behaviors, that, left alone, emerge all by themselves.

And our contention, born of decades of deep experience with bureaucracies, is that nurturing and protecting what is natural and healthy in an organization is far more effective than curing what is unhealthy in that organization.

The bottom line of this book: monster bureaucracies suck at innovation, but such monsters can still benefit from innovation if they conspicuously avoid tromping on it or chewing it up when it sprouts up around them.

One more thing before we get started...

This book tells the stories of five innovators who catalyzed the creation of game-changing technologies.

We use the term "catalyze" because the innovators we profile didn't necessarily do all of — or even most of — the heavy lifting to elevate important new technologies to new levels. Rather, in different ways, each of these innovators, by analogy, ignited a spark that caught fire, or kept someone else's fragile spark from being snuffed out so that it could eventually catch fire.

We offer this insight because a major theme of this book is that innovation is a team sport requiring personal, often informal, bonds among diverse groups of people, and we don't want to leave the impression, even by implication, that heroic actions by single individuals changed the world.

When it comes to innovation, especially in big bureaucracies, it truly does ... take a village.

Chapter 1:
Give the monster all the credit

Baqubah Iraq, March 2007

At exactly 3:00 AM a dog barking next door woke Abdul (not his real name), bringing him instantly awake. Sleeping fully dressed on an old, smelly mattress, with counterfeit Nikes on his feet, Abdul wrapped his hand around the cold steel of his banana-clipped AK-47. As had been his habit the last few months, he'd been sleeping on the flat roof of his brother's house, next to the coop that housed his brother's carrier pigeons.

Creeping low, AK in hand, Abdul made his way to the roof's edge and permitted himself a quick look to the street below. There was no moon, and a power outage, frequent in the area since 2003, kept the street dark. But something had made the usually taciturn dog start barking.

There it was, the slightest movement, black against black. Then another furtive movement, and another. He imagined that he heard static from a radio.

The black-clad Americans had found him, and his brother.

What to do? He'd been arrested two years earlier and released for reasons he couldn't fathom and was still alive because he'd surrendered peacefully then.

Should he give up without a fight now, too?

Heart racing, he took a deep breath and tried to think through the odds. The Americans were getting good at surrounding their prey before pouncing, so his chances of escaping—becoming what he'd learned the Americans liked to call a squirter—were slim.

He could spray the street with weapon's fire before leaping onto a neighbor's roof, but a nearby sniper might take him out. Chances were excellent he was in a sniper's sight at that very moment. He peered into the night at the roofs of houses around him in the crowded neighborhood, looking for a glint from the optics of an American sniper's scope or night vision goggles, or maybe a flash of green from the goggles' display screens.

Seeing nothing on neighboring rooftops, retreating from his own roof's edge, Abdul concluded that—glint or no glint, flash of green or no, he was probably being watched. He looked up involuntarily, straining his hearing to pick up the telltale whine from a predator drone's engine above. It wasn't his imagination: faint engine noise rode on the pre-dawn air.

Maybe sleeping on the roof to make a quick escape onto an adjoining roof hadn't been such a good idea.

Reaching a decision, Abdul put down his AK. They would interrogate him and put him on trial, and might execute him for what he'd done, but probably not. The shifting sands of Iraqi politics and Iraqi-American relations had stopped more than a few of his colleagues from being hanged or shot, and some, like him, had even been released.

And Abdul didn't hate the Americans as much as most did. He was fervently opposed to their occupation, but on the plus side it had provided steady income to him and his brother as IED bomb-makers for years now. Truth be told, they were financially far better off now than under Saddam and the Baath party.

Abdul kneeled, facing the door to the narrow stairway leading from the second floor to the roof, placing his arms behind his neck, hoping the snipers or the drone above — or both — would report his surrender before the Americans killed him. He wondered how the Americans had found him.

Had a jealous neighbor or member of a rival tribe reported him? The electronics seller who supplied him parts? A rival bomb-maker wishing to eliminate a competitor? He'd long ago abandoned his cell phone, so it couldn't be that.

What in Allah's name was it?

The unblinking eye in the sky

The name of the thing that netted Abdul and his brother in a counter-IED sweep targeting a network of bomb-makers in Baqubah, a hub of such activity, was an airborne surveillance system called Constant Hawk.

Constant Hawk was an Army operated aerial surveillance system that collected very high-resolution imagery over a very wide field of view, enabling it to capture and store very detailed images of huge swaths of terrain below. Manned aircraft carrying the surveillance system would fly back and forth over an area of interest such as Baghdad, or Baqubah, for many hours, collecting vast amounts of imagery for later analysis. [1,2,3,4]

Constant Hawk Aircraft at Maryland Proving Ground, 2006

The Department of Defense (DOD) developed the system to counter improvised explosive devices (IEDs) that were killing or wounding vast numbers of coalition forces in Iraq and Afghanistan.

Thus, Constant Hawk had powerful software designed not only to find IEDs before they exploded, but also to locate the people who were building, planting, and triggering the explosive devices.

After a long mission, the manned aircraft carrying the behemoth digital camera and its recorded imagery

would land, the data offloaded and given to analysis
who would pore over the imagery looking for IED-related events.

At the heart of the special software were algorithms
for change detection that could alert an analyst to con-
ditions that had changed from one recording to the
next. Disturbed earth next to a heavily traveled road,
for example, would suggest that a new IED had just
been planted there. Once a suspicious location was
identified, a bomb disposal team could be sent there to
disarm and retrieve the device for forensic analysis. [4]

In a sense, Constant Hawk was a time machine that
let the Army peer into the future, seeing looming IED
incidents before they occurred.

As valuable as looking into the future was, traveling
back in time was even more useful. For instance, once
suspicious disturbed earth was discovered, analysts
could scroll back in time, hitting rewind if you will, to
track-back which vehicles had stopped at or near that
site, then follow those vehicles back in time to their origin, say a house 10 miles away. Rewinding further, analysts could then track previous vehicle and foot traffic
to and from that house of interest, to learn the points of
origin of those who came and went there, tracking back
to other locations, and so forth, like unraveling a long,
tangled thread. [1,2,3,4,5,6]

With this powerful capability, Constant Hawk could
systematically identify individuals who triggered bombs,
planted bombs, supplied bombs, built bombs (for ex-

ample, Abdul) and even, in some cases, funded the IED network. In other words, to roll-up the entire supply chain of IED activity.

The Constant Hawk system received a number of DOD awards, and was widely regarded as a game-changing innovation in the campaign against IEDs.

More important, it saved a lot of lives on the battle-field.

How Constant Hawk got off the ground

Many different players, inside and outside the government, contributed to Constant Hawk's success, including the IED Defeat Task Force, Lawrence Livermore National Labs, Army Research Labs, EOIR Technologies, L3 Communications, and Jorge Scientific, to name just a few.

But nowhere in public (or even not-so-public) accounts of Constant Hawk's creation and deployment will you find the name of Brian Hibbeln. Brian likes it that way because his astonishing track record of success accelerating new technology for DOD depends upon him NOT taking credit for his stealthy work. Brian told us, "If you are above the radar and looking to get credit for your successes, someone will try to shoot you."

We're not talking stealthy in the sense of keeping his work classified, which was often necessary, but stealthy in the sense of letting other people bask in the spotlight of successes that Brian catalyzed.

For Brian was a catalyst of innovation in the true

sense of the meaning of a chemical catalyst. Like a catalyst, he accelerated "chemical reactions" without ever being found in the end-product of those reactions. Think of his influence as meat tenderizer containing enzymes to catalyze the breakdown of muscle tissues in meat without actually being part of the meat itself. Hibbeln meat-tenderized many hard-to-chew innovations so that they could later be digested by the warfighters who needed them.

The way Brian helped Constant Hawk come into being is a textbook example of how he worked, and a fabulous illustration of why informal machinations based on personal relationships are so important for innovation.

Brian Hibbeln

In the early 2000s, Brian worked in an obscure part of the Office of the Secretary of Defense (some would say, purposely obscure). He was focused on developing quick reaction technology to help warfighters in Iraq and Afghanistan.

At the time Brian worked for Principal Deputy Assistant Secretary of Defense Chuck Perkins, partnering with other parts of DOD and IC on Advanced Concept Technology Demonstrations (ACTDs).

One such concept demonstrator was a persistent surveillance airborne platform to counter IEDs. The Army Research Labs (ARL) believed these might be feasible for the first time because of advances in high resolution digital cameras, cheap and abundant digital memory to store detailed images on an aircraft, and new image change detection software to automatically call analyst's attention to small details that changed in imagery over time. John Eicke and Andrew Ladas of ARL presented this idea at a regular Thursday dinner meeting that Brian hosted for one of his many "special customers" (special, meaning, don't ever ask who they are).

But as is often the case in DOD circles, warfighters — such as Brian's "special customers" — don't know how to move promising new technologies out of the laboratory and onto the battlefield. That giant leap across the valley of death requires working through a lot of Pentagon red tape, a lot of money, and connections with other people in the Pentagon responsible for official requirements generation and procurement.

Put another way, all that Pentagon bureaucratic stuff requires a Brian Hibbeln, a Zen Master of pushing the right buttons, pulling the right levers, being persistent, and whispering in the right ears inside the Pentagon.

One of the "ears" Brian whispered in after learning of the airborne persistent surveillance idea belonged to Chuck Perkins, who suggested that his office chip in $2 million of the initial $20M required to test and field the system, code named Constant Hawk.

At first glance, it might seem that providing funds far below the required $20 million was somewhat miserly, and worse, leave the embryonic Constant Hawk project fatally underfunded.

But in the weird logic of Washington, providing the entire $20 million would have permanently grounded Constant Hawk. Had he done so, all of the different players required to make the project a reality and to operate and use its products would not have placed any value upon it and never used it.

In behavioral science, this phenomenon is called cognitive dissonance, a fancy way of saying that we only value things we have to sacrifice for or pay for. The classic example is a teenager's first car. If the parent gifts the car to their kid, the teen likely won't apply the effort to take care of it: washing it, servicing it, and above all, driving it carefully to avoid damage.

But if the teenager has to come up with most of the money for the car themselves by mowing lawns or taking after-school jobs—with only some help from their parents—they will probably care for the automobile lovingly and drive more carefully.

And so when those teenagers grow up and become adults working in the Defense Department, they must "feel some pain" and contribute hard-fought-for dollars in their budgets in order to psychologically embrace a new concept.

Thus, Brian took Chuck's $2 million and started a kitty, persuading other organizations who would bene-fit from Constant Hawk to chip in a few million here and a few million there, until the full $20 million had been collected. Part of Brian's successful pitch to such investors (or bettors, if you will) was that he, Brian, would do all the bureaucratic heavy lifting, getting offi-cial requirements documents issued, working with the procurement part of the Pentagon to buy the different components, get a suitable aircraft to carry the cam-era and memory, etc. And Brian's small team would also develop the all-important concept of operations (CONOPS) required for all military systems that speci-fied the who, what, where, when, and why of Constant Hawk operation on the battlefield.

The team Brian pulled together included:

- an aircraft and aircrew

- image analysts to detect IED-related activities

- a team to build and install the hardware

- testing (e.g., operating, maintenance costs, and aircrew time)

- flight operations (e.g., operating, maintenance costs, and aircrew time)

Less than a year later, after a successful flight test in Wisconsin, Constant Hawk was sent to Iraq. A few months after that, the bomb maker Abdul and his brother were successfully net in a counter-IED operation.

How Brian got to be Brian

What kind of person works hard at networking, raising money, cutting through red tape, and writing dry, dull CONOPS, all just to give other people credit for his efforts?

What kind of person becomes legendary in Washington for not being famous?

In Brian's case, one who grew up gay in the Midwest in a family of farmers who were anything but sympathetic to gays.

As the oldest child with a farmer-turned-engineer father, Brian felt that he never lived up to his parents' high expectations, even when he secured a prestigious appointment in the Air Force Academy and became an Air Force Officer.

Later, while still in the Air Force, getting his master degree in engineering physics, Brian finally came out to his mother, who was less than pleased, saying, "You're not going to tell your father are you?"

So, Brian's early years were spent as an outsider in his midwestern community, in his family, and certainly in the US Military, which had later instituted the don't-ask-don't-tell policy that would have gotten Brian discharged the second he revealed his sexuality.

When we asked Brian whether growing up an outsider motivated him later to form strong bonds and become a consummate networker, he paused and said, "I never thought about it that way, but yes, that's probably why, and it makes sense."

It wasn't the first time that such a question caused Brian to do some introspection and soul-searching.

Once, on a covert military aircraft flying to an undisclosed location to meet with "special customers," one of the authors of this book watched Brian scowl over his Blackberry, which was glitching in some way.

"What's wrong, Brian?" Haseltine asked.

"Oh, my IT guy says my contact list is probably screwing this thing up."

"How can a contact list cause a malfunction? It's just a flat file, dumb data with no malware."

"I've exceeded the maximum number of contacts, apparently, causing something like a buffer overflow." Brian explained. "I think 5,000 is the limit."

Haseltine came back, "Why Brian, you're what Malcom Gladwell calls a super-connector. Admit it. Fess up."

"Nah," Brian retorted. "Not really."

But after the flight, Brian realized that he actually was a super-connector, in every sense of the word.

More importantly, Brian's realization gave him a new lease on life, a new raison d'être.

"That insight on the plane to [redacted] saved me from a midlife crisis I was having at the time," Brian said. "I wasn't sure where to go next in my life and career, but I realized I should continue and do what I'm apparently really good at."

And continue to connect Brian did, working his behind-the-scenes magic in the Pentagon for another 14 years, giving birth to one game-changing innovation after another until he left government service at the end of 2020 to work full time as a venture capitalist.

Brian's departure was an incalculable loss to the Pentagon, but Brian being Brian, his change of career will doubtless be only harbinger of more game-changing innovations to come in the commercial sector.

References

1. "Wikipedia, Constant Hawk," Wikimedia Foundation, last modified July 27, 2020, 20:39, https://en.wikipedia.org/wiki/Constant Hawk

2. "Constant Hawk – Afghanistan (CH-A)," *GlobalSecurity.org*, accessed April 14, 2021, https://www.globalsecurity.org/intell/systems/constant-hawk.htm

3. Brandon Pollachek, "Eyes in the Sky providing more than 5000 hours of coverage a month," *US Army* (website), September 11, 2017, https://www.army.mil/article/193634/eyes_in_the_sky_providing_more_than_5000_hours_of_coverage_a_month

4. Defense Industry Daily staff, "Walking Back the Cat: The US Army's Constant Hawk," *Defense Industry Daily* (website), October 2, 2011, https://www.defenseindustrydaily.com/walking-back-the-cat-the-us-armys-constant-hawk-06832/

5. "Night Eyes for the Constant Hawk – Opening the night for Counter-IED Surveillance," *Defense Update* (website), September 17, 2009, https://defense-update.com/20090917_awapss.html

6. A. Butler, "U.S. Army Emarss, Constant Hawk efforts move forward," *ResearchGate* (website), October 2010, https://www.researchgate.net/publication/287412637_US_Army_Emarss_Constant_Hawk_efforts_move_forward

Chapter 2:
Don't wait for monsters

Charlotte, Iowa 2004

Horse owner Bev Holzrichter was in trouble. Sierra, a frightened mare in Bev's stables who was struggling to give birth to a foal, had kicked Bev three times in the chest, causing internal bleeding, hypothermia, shock, and imminent death.

Fortunately for Bev, she had set up a live stream for global horse lovers to watch Sierra's labor. As Bev lay stunned and dying in her stable, viewers in Germany, France, and the UK called the local rescue squad in Charlotte, Iowa, who showed up just in time to save Bev's life.

Bev later said, "The internet is my hero. Those people watching are the ones who helped me. If it weren't for the technology of the webcam, I'm not sure when I would have been found or what would have happened to me."

The internet site where we found this story, titled *The Internet Saved My Life*, carried nine other compelling examples of how the internet has not only changed our lives, but, in some cases, *saved* them.

- A 40-year-old German tourist lost on an ice floe was rescued when a viewer of a web-cam streaming the ice floe spotted him and called authorities.

- A leukemia sufferer in India got a life-saving bone marrow donation after posting on social media.

- A man recovering from ankle surgery goo-gled his symptoms of chest pain and breath-ing difficulty, discovered he probably had a pulmonary embolism, and called 911 just in time.

- An Atlanta politician who found a woman suffering a heart attack had just enough juice left in his cell phone to tweet a request for res-cue.

It's fitting that these life and death stories featured rescues triggered by informal observers because the internet itself emerged from a highly informal, catch-as-catch-can process that began in the late 1960s. Although the internet has become a bastion of winner-take-all, highly formal and ultra-wealthy mega-corporations such as Amazon, Facebook, and Google, not to mention government websites, remote learning, and other highly organized activities, the rag-tag group of computer scientists who got the mammoth net started were anything but wealthy and organized.

In fact, many of them were low-status, low-paid graduate students. Because they didn't know any better, they laid the foundations for the modern internet by literally making things up as they went. In fact, the manner in which they made things up became the standard-making process for how the internet evolved.

Steve Crocker, a lowly UCLA graduate student, wrote the first "Request for Comment" (RFC #1) memo that set in motion the evolution of internet standards that we use to this very day. His story illustrates the formidable power of the informal in fostering game-changing innovation.

A pre-Watergate break-in

Two high school kids from Van Nuys, California, a valley community of northern Los Angeles, discussed how to circumvent a big obstacle that stood between them and their computer science ambitions.

It was a Saturday in 1961 on the campus of UCLA, and the two students—Steve and Vint—wanted to get weekend access to a computer they had been using to explore the behavior of a transcendental function. Steve was taking courses at UCLA in parallel with finishing high school, and had been hanging out around the computers on campus.

The obstacle in question was a locked door to the engineering building housing the Bendix G-15 minicomputer, the object of their desire.

It was Saturday and very few people were around. The situation seemed hopeless. Vint and Steve stood looking at the building. Vint noticed the second-floor casement window was open. "We're not really going to do this," thought Steve, but Vint climbed up on Steve's shoulders and crawled through the open window. In minute he reappeared at the building's door.

The institutional door to the building opened with a push bar. The building was empty and they could work all day without interruption. Looking ahead to lunchtime, they taped the door so they could leave and return.

Eleven years later, the Watergate burglars were caught when a plain-clothed guard found a similar door taped open. By then Steve was living in Washington, working for the US Department of Defense, carrying a top-secret security clearance. "When I read the news, quite a shiver ran down my spine," said Steve.

The awesome power of informality

Those familiar with the very early history of the internet will recognize Steve and Vint as the now famous PhD computer scientists and internet pioneers Steve Crocker and Vint Cerf.

This tale of teenage breaking-and-entering is well known in certain geeky circles (and has become legend).

However, despite the lore, Steve's boosting Vint to the second-floor window is not the origin of the computer term bootstrapping (the process by which computers literally bring themselves to life, by their bootstraps, as it were). That term had already been around for at least a decade before their escapade.

But what is true about their story is how innovators — and there is no question about the massive impact of the innovations Steve and Vint brought about in their storied careers — think about things and approach problems. When confronted with obstacles, innovators don't go home. They go around the obstacles. And oh, by the way, in going around obstacles, it is often wise not to stand on formality, but instead to stand on the shoulders of a co-conspirator.

Vint Cerf (left) and Steve Crocker (right) at Vint's wedding in 1966

The story you are about to read, Steve Crocker's story, can be summed up, really, in the vignette of breaking into the computer lab that long ago Saturday. To innovate (i.e., get into a locked building) the most important ingredients are, (1) a disrespect for formality, and (2) the right personal relationships, at the right time, in the right place.

How the internet got started and Steve's role in it

The network that revolutionized just about everything humans do—from communicating to dating to shopping to banking to watching TV shows, not to mention controlling military operations—began in the US Department of Defense. You might think that because the internet started in the world's largest bureaucracy that it emerged through an organized, gradual, highly bureaucratic, highly formal process.

But you'd be wrong. The very first Defense Department-sponsored meeting of the "Network Working Group," tasked with establishing a way for an embryonic network of geographically separated computers to communicate with each other, was—despite being crucial for the ultimate creation of the modern internet— anything but formal.

But before describing that all-important first meeting, it will be useful to summarize the events that made it necessary.

A little internet pre-history

In the mid-1960s, the Defense Department's ARPA (Advanced Research Projects Agency, now DARPA) was funding a number of separate computer science projects at universities such as Stanford, UCLA, UC Santa Barbara, and the University of Utah. Computers on different campuses each focused on a separate discipline: some focused on advanced graphics, some on user interfaces, and some on AI.

But the ARPA office director for much of this work, Bob Taylor, was frustrated that it took a lot of his time to remotely log in to each of these ARPA-funded computers in order to work on them. Each computer required its own dedicated remote terminal and login procedure, and the computers were completely isolated from each other.

What Taylor wanted was a way to make his job of working with all those widely separated computers easier. What Taylor wanted was a single login to a single terminal to access all of the widely dispersed computers at one time.

Taylor also wanted to save ARPA money by allowing ARPA-funded computer scientists to remotely use existing ARPA-funded computers rather than spending ARPA money on their own, completely new computers.

It wasn't the first time in the history of science and technology, nor the last, that the simple urge to save time and money, rather than any formal grand vision of the future, triggered what would ultimately become a revolution.

Anyhow, in 1966, Bob Taylor convinced ARPA director Charlie Herzfield to give him a million dollars to connect ARPA-funded machines across the country. Taylor used the money to pay the Cambridge, MA, company Bolt Beranek and Newman (BBN), to design and build what we now call a router (back then they called it an Interface Message Processor — or IMP) to connect the different computer systems together. Four computer sites at UCLA, Stanford Research Institute (SRI), UC Santa Barbara, and University of Utah were selected to be the first "nodes" on the fledgling network.

By the summer of 1968, procurement for the IMPs was initiated. The IMPs and the long-distance lines that would connect them would form the basic communication substrate of the network, but further work was needed to organize what the computers at each site would say to each other.

The ARPA office asked SRI to convene a meeting among the four sites to bring the communication protocols into existence.

Mind you, at the time, this nascent networking effort was not viewed as high priority by most of the four labs (except Kleinrock's at UCLA) because each of the labs had its own focus or passion, be it on human interfaces (Doug Englebart at SRI who developed the mouse, the desktop, and other user interface breakthroughs) or computer graphics (Ivan Sutherland at the University of Utah who developed real-time computer graphics that power every video game today).

Thus, the task of working out how the four computers were going to talk to one another was delegated to low level lab workers, which, as anyone who has ever toiled in academia knows, is another name for ... graduate students.

And in 1968, the two graduate students representing the UCLA lab were none other than ... Steve Crocker and Vint Cerf.

After finishing undergraduate work at different schools, Vint and Steve were now graduate students in the nascent UCLA computer science program working with Professors Gerald Estrin and Leonard Kleinrock.

Dr. Leonard Kleinrock of UCLA, who had pioneered the mathematics of digital packets that would later serve as a foundational principle of internet communications, was something of an exception to the group of ARPA academic principal investigators. He was highly motivated to make a network of research computers across the country a reality. But because his computer science colleagues at other universities did not view networking as a priority, Kleinrock said, "I met with reluctance. No one was eager to share their computer resources with others on the Net. I did some serious arm-twisting."

Partly as a result of Kleinrock's arm twisting, the academics agreed to send representatives to the first meeting of what would later be called the Network Working Group. In August 1968, Steve and Vint hopped in a car and drove from Westwood up the 101 Freeway to UC Santa Barbara where the meeting was to take place.

At the time of the first meeting, ARPA had just decided how it wanted to connect the first four nodes on the so-called ARPANET, releasing specifications for an Interface Message Processor (IMP) that was to "glue" the network together.

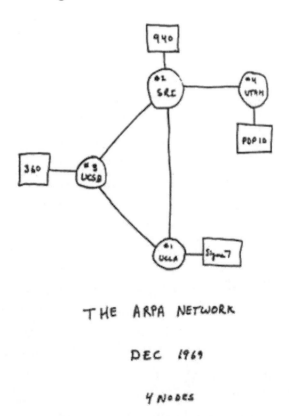

THE ARPA NETWORK

DEC 1969

4 NODES

This early diagram of the first version of ARPANET (notice how formal it looks) illustrates the challenge that Steve, Vint, and the other graduate students and low-level investigators were to take up in the first meeting.

Each square in the sketch represented the computer that already existed at each of the four labs: A Sigma 7 at UCLA, an IBM 360 at UCSB, SDS 940 at Stanford Research Institute, and a DEC PDP 10 at the University of Utah.

The four computers were wildly different from one another, yet each circle in the sketch represented identical IMPs (or routers) that translated digital packets into a form that each of the four different computers could understand.

So the goal of the Santa Barbara meeting was to start figuring out how to get the four computers hundreds of miles apart, each with different operating systems, machine instruction sets, and even "word lengths" (e.g., 24 bits, 32 bits, 36 bits — modern computers are usually 64 bits), to talk to each other.

The task was similar to figuring out how to get four people who each only speak one language — say English, Russian, Chinese, and Swahili — to communicate in ways all four can not only understand, but understand perfectly, with zero errors. (Computers then, as now, are not very forgiving of even small mistakes in vocabulary or grammar.)

This task was considered so difficult, even absurd,

that ARPA could only find a few brave companies (BBN among them) to even consider designing and building the IMPs.

The very first Network Working Group meeting

With this in mind, the meeting's organizer, Elmer Shapiro of SRI, kicked off the meeting, outlining its ambitious goals and laying out some ideas for establishing network communication protocols for the group to consider.

Steve Crocker said that, by and large, the assembled group were cool to these ideas, and what followed proceeded more like a loosely organized cocktail party than a Defense Department sponsored and funded meeting. At this "cocktail party" small groups of like-minded people found each other in a process Steve calls "self-selection." Bonds of respect formed in these small groups proved crucial to what was to follow the next several years, and to the future of the internet itself.

As the meeting drew to a close, no firm conclusions or agreements had been reached, but a group of "about 12 of us," according to Crocker, agreed that, (1) they all need to keep talking, and (2) frequent travel to each of the four labs by the groups would be necessary for everyone to understand the big picture. Steve doesn't remember who first coined the phrase, but it was universally agreed to:

"Before the bits can travel, our butts must travel."

Steve interjected at this point in the interview with him (at a Chinese Restaurant in Silver Spring Maryland), that "It was so ironic that, due to our very limited travel budget, we desperately needed the very network we were trying to create."

Traveling butts and the Little Garden

Budgets notwithstanding, members of the group did travel and meet often, visiting labs, learning how each other's host computers worked, and discussing how to get all the machines to talk to one another.

Usually, when the group visited SRI, they ate dinner at a Szechuan restaurant in Palo Alto called "The Little Garden." And although the meetings at SRI were somewhat productive, the *real* work, where the greatest progress was made — according to Steve — were animated conversations over chop sticks, sweet and sour pork, General Tso Chicken, and egg rolls in the Little Garden. Ideas flew fast and furious, sketches were quickly drawn and discarded on paper napkins. And personal bonds among researchers at widely separated labs were forged and strengthened.

Steve summed up the importance of those Little Garden Chinese dinners this way, "All the conversations that started the network, began at that place."

It's worth pausing the narrative here to make a point about the Little Garden. The restaurant was hardly what the hyper-rigid, hyper-formal Defense Department had in mind as the place where "all the conversations" to start the network would take place.

But we would argue that those vitally important conversations didn't happen *despite* taking place after work over egg noodles and hot tea—instead of during the workday inside a conference room—but *precisely because* they took place outside a formal setting.

Think about your own experience: how many giant leaps forward in your work, where sparks flew and excitement ran rampant, occurred in scheduled meetings in conference rooms lit with harsh fluorescent lights versus in chance encounters in hallways, bathrooms, at company picnics, restaurants, bars, trade shows, or conventions?

Our guess is very few, if any.

Why? Because formality kills innovation, while informality breeds it.

We'll explore the reasons why this is true in greater depth later, but the rest of Steve's story will further illustrate the vital importance of informal human emotional bonds in laying the foundation for game-changing breakthroughs like the internet.

Time to act like an adult: using lessons from childhood

As 1968 turned into 1969, meetings of the working groups progressed at the four sites. Nothing formal had been written down yet to document the conclusions the group had reached. "We were making things up as we went," Steve explained, "and no one was telling us how to do what we were trying to do, or even what, exactly, to produce. We kept waiting for some grown-up from the east [the Pentagon or Boston] to direct us, but that never happened."

As much as he valued the group's work and enjoyed Chinese food, Steve started to get uneasy in the spring of 1969 because he sensed that the time for unchecked informality, although incredibly productive, was fast coming to an end. With the completion of IMP hardware months away, the time had come to actually produce results.

Steve's instinct was that the right approach to codifying the group's work would live in a sweet spot that occupied a space somewhere between too much and too little organization and formality.

This instinct grew out of experiences putting together informal groups a decade earlier, in high school.

A product of a broken home who shuttled between parents in California and Illinois, Steve always felt isolated as a kid, and uncomfortable with all the "social stuff" that other kids did. Steve's main company growing up were math books that he pored over, learning as much as he could about the exciting field.

But Steve did value companionship, and so developed a close relationship with high school classmate Vint Cerf, who shared Steve's passion for math. And Vint, as someone with a hearing disability, also could be perceived as something of an outsider. One of Steve and Vint's ideas was to form a math club at their high school to include like-minded students.

Steve took the lead setting up the club, learning from the boys' vice principal what was needed to get a charter, and leading discussions among early group members about how the club should run itself. "It took us over a year to come up with a constitution," Steve said, "during which time we did very little math, instead spending all our time anticipating problems that may or may not ever happen."

As a consequence of wasting so much time getting agreement on formal math club rules, when Steve was president of the nascent UCLA computer club, he opted for the least amount of formality.

"For some reason," Steve observed, "when I get in groups, I am the one that ends up writing things down, and so it was, almost a decade later, I was the one who took up the task of codifying the Network Working Group's conclusions."

But in taking on this task, Steve's belief from founding his high school club was that he needed to find a sweet spot between too little and too much formality.

And he thought a lot about what he should call the document, and what it should contain, fearing that whatever he did would be cast in concrete prematurely, or that, at long last, someone official from back east would show up and say, "No, you can't do it that way."

So Steve applied the lightest touch possible, eschewing the "this is how it's going to be" approach typical of government specifications, requirements documents, Request for Proposals (RFPs), etc. Instead, he employed, at the suggestion of Network Working Group member, Bill Duval, the humble title of Request for Comments (RFC). This title proclaimed loudly that the document was not the end, but the beginning of a specification, that the ultimate answer would not come from tight-fisted top-down command and control, but from loosey-goosey, bottoms-up collaboration.

Steve's first draft, RFC 1, therefore, was more of a plan for a plan, than a plan itself. Something that others could add to, subtract from, and flesh out to ensure that the end result met their labs' needs. The title of RFC 1 was simply "Network Software," and it outlined a broad framework for the code that was to run on the four IMPs, gluing the network together.

As of this writing, there are now 8,650 RFCs managed by the descendent of the Network Working Group, the Internet Engineering Task Force (IETF). As with RFC 1, the documents define the standards of the internet.

Purists will argue that ARPANET, which RFC 1 sought to bootstrap into existence, was not actually the internet because it was only one small network, not a *network of networks*, which is the defining attribute of the INTERNET.

But that's like saying a fertilized egg is not the adult human grown from that egg: literally true, but missing the larger point.

No egg, no adult. No RFC1, no internet.

In other words, Steve's contribution—RFC 1— stands as one of the seminal moments in internet history, not so much because of what it did (set in motion standards creation for the internet) but for what it *didn't do*: proscriptively choke the life out of a fragile, necessarily collaborative, necessarily informal process.

That is not to say that the contribution of others, including Cerf, Kleinrock, Postel, Kahn, Taylor and his ARPANET lead Larry Roberts, and many others, weren't equally or more important. They were.

But Steve's RFC1 did much more than build a skeleton on which the flesh of the modern internet would hang: it set the informal tone, the all-important point of view for how the collaborators who would create the mother-of-all collaboration tools would *themselves* collaborate.

As such, RFC1, despite all the digital jargon in it, was less about technology than about human social behavior: innovation-spawning cooperative behavior that flourishes with informal human bonds of trust and respect forged over Chinese food, not social behavior taking place in stuffy, harshly lit conference rooms over bad coffee and stale donuts.

We can only wonder what the fortune cookies broken open by Steve and others at the Little Garden all those many years ago foretold. But we can be sure that many *more* fortune cookies, at many *more* Chinese Restaurants, remain to be broken open by those with the courage to invent the future.

Chapter 3:
Harness full monster power

A chance meeting in the quad

As soon as Disney's VP for Advanced Development Mike Goslin left the air-conditioned comfort of his innovation lab for a short walk in the blistering San Fernando valley heat to have lunch in the cafeteria, he spotted a former co-worker walking across the quad into the Disney Burbank consumer products headquarters building a few dozen yards away.

Mike had kept in touch with the colleague over the years, occasionally chatting over coffee about their shared passion, virtual worlds and virtual reality (VR). The two had come to respect and trust each other. Even though they now worked for different companies, they informally helped each other with introductions to useful contacts and with informal counsel on business problems.

"Carter," Mike called out as he changed directions and hurried over to his old colleague. "What brings you back to the Mouse?"

15 years earlier, Carter Agar had been the Busi-

ness Development lead in Asia for Disney's first on-line multiplayer game, Toon Town Online, when Mike had led the project. Carter stopped and turned to greet Mike. Tilting his head towards the headquarters building, he said, "Trying to negotiate a license for one of our products."

Mike nodded. "You still at Lenovo?"

"Yep. What are you up to these days?"

Mike grinned. "Remember how I said I wanted to get back into consumer VR? Well, my group here has started developing some cool new stuff. You should drop by to see it next time you're in town."

"Sounds like a plan," Carter said, checking his watch. "Gotta run. Let's talk when I get back to the office."

Mike's follow up call came a few weeks later and included Carter's boss, Jason Huang, the head of consumer R&D at Lenovo. That call kicked off a whirlwind collaboration between Disney and Lenovo that moved at breathtaking speed, putting a top selling augmented reality experience on the shelves at Best Buy in time for Christmas, a scant 18 months after Mike and Carter's chance encounter.

The Lenovo/Disney Augmented Reality System (Star Wars-themed Jedi Challenges and Marvel-themed Marvel Dimension of Heroes) dominated the market for head-worn augmented reality for over three years.

Lenovo and Disney together spent just a few million dollars to quickly bring a killer product to market, beating competitors who outspent them by multiples of hundreds (if not thousands), and they did so in months rather than years. So just how did they do it? Further, how did these multi-billion megaliths come to act like scrappy Silicon Valley start-ups to beat a company who *was* a start-up (Magic Leap)?

Lenovo/Disney Augmented Reality System

The story begins in Tallahassee, Florida, 40 years before Mike and Carter bumped into each other that fateful day in Burbank.

This world is boring: I'd rather invent my own

Graduate students Michael and Evelyn Goslin returned from classes at the University of Florida to their apartment in Tallahassee, only to discover that it had been taken over by a 45-pound spider.

Giant web filaments crisscrossed the entire living room a foot above the floor. They vibrated gently in the breeze from the ever-present air conditioning. Beneath the web, the creature that had spun the vast web lay on its back, holding nearby filaments as he regarded the newcomers.

Evelyn addressed the enormous arachnid: "What are you doing?"

Six-year-old Mike Goslin finished tying up another junction of the yarn he'd hijacked, putting the finishing touches on his creation.

"I'm a spider, and this is my web. I live *here* now."

Evelyn and Michael senior exchanged a look, not the first of its kind, and far from the last. Their son Michael Paul Goslin was easily bored and forever inventing new ways to entertain himself.

"I always thought that worlds I created were more interesting than the one I actually inhabited," Mike would later say. "So the only way I could stave off boredom was to create new places and experiences."

Mike Goslin as a 6-year-old arachnid

As a child, Mike's penchant for creating new environments where he could escape boredom frequently put him at odds with rules laid down by others — like parents. He learned to find new ways of getting around those rules without getting in trouble. "My parents laid down the law on tree houses," Mike said, to explain his approach to creative rule breaking. "They said, 'No structures higher than 10 feet.' So I obeyed the law, making a tree house 10 feet off the ground, which did a great job of masking from view another that I built much higher in the same tree."

Later, in college, when Mike's friends held an annual Mad Hatter party, he built huge paper mache caterpillars and other characters from Alice in Wonderland.

But I was always disappointed because the fantasy characters and worlds I created never quite matched up to the vision of them that I had in my mind. Until, one day, while trying to figure out what to do with my life and career after getting my degree in Psychology from Duke, I read an article about this new thing called virtual reality. What intrigued me was that with VR, you could build anything you might imagine with 3D graphics, exactly the way you imagined it because you were no longer constrained by physical reality.

Excited about VR, Mike arranged through a friend to get an interview with a brand-new, Army-funded simulation institute at the University of Central Florida (UCF) where VR research would figure prominently in the research program.

There was just one problem: the rules for being accepted into the new program required applicants to have a computer science degree.

Well-practiced at circumventing—if not breaking—rules to escape the boring "real" world, Mike hit upon a scheme to push his way into virtual reality.

"Look," he told the UCF interviewers, "at the end of the day, everything you do here is meant to benefit humans, not machines. So you're going to need people skilled in Psychology—like me—to translate what you create into things that humans can actually use." Getting no immediate response, Mike added, "So when can I start?"

Apparently sharing the ancient Roman's belief that "audacity triumphs over veracity," the project lead, after a moment's thought answered, "I don't know, when *can* you start?"

Mike immediately enrolled in computer science classes, eventually getting a master's degree and landing a job at Walt Disney Imagineering's Virtual Reality Studio, which was working on Disney's first VR theme park attraction, Aladdin's Magic Carpet Ride.

At Disney's VR studio, Mike finally had the tools to create experiences that matched the excitement of what he could imagine. And despite a continued penchant for breaking rules, Mike rose steadily through the ranks, eventually becoming a vice president in charge of online virtual worlds.

Mike took a break from Disney in 2009, starting up his own VR and gaming companies, until he got a call to return to Disney in 2013 to become creative lead on a project that had been set in motion a couple years earlier by another unconventional thinker, the Chairman of Disney Consumer Products, Bob Chapek.

Something new at the Mouse House

With a degree in microbiology, Bob Chapek was something of an anomaly at Disney.

Bob had an MBA from a top school like other senior executives at Disney. However, when considering novel business ideas, his early passion for science and answering big questions pre-disposed him to focus less on "the numbers" (Net Present Value, Return on Investment, and other staples of MBAs) and more on big drivers and major market forces that couldn't be reduced to meaningful numbers.

Bob would sometimes frustrate his financial executives by giving big ideas priority over big numbers, backing projects that, at first glance, didn't pencil out.

One such endeavor was a transportation initiative for Walt Disney World in Orlando, called Skyliner, that would let guests remain inside the "Disney Bubble" while moving between experiences at the mega-resort, instead of breaking the magic spell by getting in a rental car or ride share service. Although the financial analysts could not imagine how the proposed investment in new transportation systems would pay off, Bob believed that preserving the Disney Bubble was an important way to differentiate Disney from competitors, and that the idea of the Bubble was bigger than the projected numbers.

He turned out to be right, as the transportation initiative that he sponsored eventually did pencil out, as guests came to appreciate the seamlessness of their Disney vacation.

Bob Chapek's approach of putting ideas ahead of numbers motivated Mike Goslin to leave the start-up world. He returned to Disney to lead a creative team in an internal start-up that Bob had green-lit in 2011 at Disney Consumer products before he was elevated to Chairman of Disney Parks and Resorts in 2015.

Bob's goal for the internal start-up, called Playmation, was to position Disney for a shift that was occurring in children's play patterns. This shift, exemplified by kids as young as two years old enjoying games and watching movies on iPads, represented a movement in the toy and play market towards "bits."

Given that the business Bob ran licensed Disney characters and franchises (think Frozen, Iron Man, Star Wars, Toy Story) to consumer companies who made and sold physical products (think toys, apparel, accessories, even orange juice), this shift offered potentially huge growth opportunities.

"As kids go more virtual," Bob said at the time,

"someone is going to innovate in that space. Why not Disney? We have the brands and the content."

But how big was the virtual play business eventually going to be? What would be its compound annual growth rate (CAGR)? What level of investments were required to capture the emerging new market? What market share could Disney anticipate? Where should Disney position itself in the value chain (in other words, make and sell products versus license franchises to others)? And above all, how much could virtual play add to Disney's overall bottom line?

Disney's historic, very disciplined approach to addressing such questions was to assemble an army of analysts and business development specialists who would posit a business model (what to sell to whom), develop a consumer proposition (what value consumers would get from virtual experiences), forecast market growth, estimate investments and returns, and calculate numbers such as CAGR, Net Present Value, Break Even Point and Internal Rate of Return. If the numbers penciled out, then Disney would invest; if the numbers didn't pencil out, they wouldn't.

This numbers-centric approach worked reasonably well for *evolutionary* changes in products and markets, and usually made sense. For virtual play, Bob's problem was that it was impossible to quantify *revolutionary* changes in products and markets for which there was no prior experience. For revolutionary products and experiences, Bob believed, it was better to ask, "Is this shift going to be big and permanent, and will Disney have any choice but to participate in it if it wants to preserve its position in children's play?"

Believing that the answer to the first question was "yes," and the second, "no," in 2011 Bob was actively seeking ways to get Disney into the virtual play business. That's when Bob Iger, Disney's CEO, asked him to meet with Haseltine, a contractor working for Disney's Corporate Planning and Business Development group under Kevin Mayer.

A year earlier, Kevin had created a corporate innovation group led by former president of TIVO, Marty Yudkovitz. Kevin tasked the group with imagining big new businesses in the white spaces of Disney, where no existing business unit currently operated. Kevin and Marty, like Bob Chapek, were looking for new products and services that were radically different from any of Disney's existing offerings.

In briefing these revolutionary concepts at quarterly innovation meetings with Bob Iger, Kevin and Marty opted for show over tell, de-emphasizing formal power point decks filled with numbers in favor of demonstrating working prototypes of radical new products. Haseltine, a former Disney Imagineer and contractor to Kevin's group, designed, built, and demonstrated the prototypes so that the Bob Iger could actually experience the new ideas, instead of trying to imagine them.

After seeing a demo of one of these new concepts, a holographic Tinker Bell playhouse that combined dynamic holographic images with physical props, Bob Iger asked Haseltine to track down Bob Chapek right away. Iger happened to know Chapek was in Team Disney, the company's headquarters building, for another meeting.

Finding Chapek one floor below Iger's office, Haseltine showed him the holographic playhouse. Bob Chapek was impressed because the concept artfully married "atoms" (the physical playhouse) with "bits" (the dynamic fairy holograms), and was a good example of what he had in mind for entering the virtual play market.

Tinker Bell Playhouse

Looking up from a fairy dancing in the air over the play set, Bob Chapek said to Haseltine, "You were an

Imagineer; did you have Imagineering build this for you?"

"No," Haseltine answered, "I did it myself in my garage."

Bob was intrigued by the demo of the holographic playhouse but was mostly impressed that the prototype had emerged from the informality of a garage instead of a more formal, well established development studio.

"I knew that, in order to go after virtual experiences, we needed to foster a garage culture," Bob said.

So Bob encouraged Haseltine to develop virtual play concepts more fully, focusing on the princess line (Belle, Ariel, Rapunzel, Cinderella, etc.), which had traditionally been a big money maker for Disney licensing.

With Kevin Mayer and Marty Yudkovizt's sponsorship, Haseltine hired a small team of writers and animators who quickly created content for a miniature child's room of the future. Its walls were animated storyboards of a day in the life of a girl who enjoyed a convergence of virtual and physical experiences. As before, he constructed the miniature room in his garage.

A few months later, Haseltine and his team showed the animating room to Bob Chapek and his top lieutenants at Consumer Products headquarters in Glendale, California.

After 5 minutes looking at the demonstration and asking questions, Bob turned to Haseltine and said, "We are going to do this."

Haseltine, who had worked for Disney for 20 years

and had participated in many number-crunching exercises that always preceded such decisions, wasn't sure he had heard Bob correctly, or that he understood what Bob meant by, "do this." He asked, "You mean we are going to actually launch a business around this concept?"

"Yes," Bob said. "First, I want you to get with my team here to work up a business plan and to expand this demo into a life size experience that we can show Bob Iger and the board of directors to get their take on it. But I'm confident we're eventually going to move ahead with this. The sooner the better."

Haseltine was thunderstruck. Having made hundreds of pitches like the one he'd just presented over a span two decades at the Mouse, he had never gotten a "yes" on the first pitch, or even heard of such a thing happening at the company. He thought "Wow, *that* was un-Disney-like." He looked at Chapek, blinking, uncomprehending, speechless, trying to get his head around what had just happened.

Chapek smiled at Haseltine's astonished look as he and his team got up to leave. "You've got lots to do; best get going."

E-magine this

Bob Chapek earmarked funds to get a full-scale demonstration of the day-in-the-life-of-a-virtual-physical-princess experience going. He assigned one of his executives, Eric Mulheim, to put together a business development and creative team and to start working "the numbers." Their job was to identify what products to develop and where investments in the new idea might yield the biggest returns.

In parallel, Haseltine assembled a technical team that, within a few months, built a full-scale bedroom featuring more than a dozen different ways that virtual-physical products could create new magic for the Disney princess franchise. There were magic tea sets, AI-driven dolls with speech recognition, animating bedroom walls, a digital magic mirror, and a printed storybook with animating images, soundtrack, and audio dialogue.

In January 2013, just a few months after funding the demo, Chapek's team demonstrated the day-in-the-life room to Bob Iger and his top leadership team, getting a positive response. Two months later, after a second demo to Disney's board of directors, a new business venture focused on virtual-physical experiences, called "E-magine," was officially launched.

As usually happens with revolutionary concepts, the path to market for "E-magine" was not a straight line. The first thing that changed was the project's name: Disney marketing decided that "Playmation" was a more suitable name for novel virtual-physical experiences. Then, in summer 2013, after Mike Goslin took over as creative lead on the project, and multiple focus groups showed that the princess franchise might not be the best fit for an initial launch, Chapek, Goslin, and the

Playmation team decided to shift focus to action play, using the Marvel Avengers franchise (such as Iron Man, Hulk, and Ultron).

A key factor in this decision was that focus groups with parents revealed growing concern that digital experiences were leading their children to become more sedentary, staying glued to screens instead of physically acting out their play fantasies. Parents wanted new play technology to get kids running around — and using their imaginations — instead of, as Mike Goslin observed, being "spoon-fed a diet of bits all the time."

So Mike Goslin got the Playmation team to focus on new experiences that motivated kids to move around their house and yard instead of staying glued to screens. After a year of inventing, tinkering, and play testing with kids, the team decided to launch with a family of wearable products and accessories built around new Internet of Things (IOT) technology. The centerpiece of the new offering was an Iron Man arm-worn "repulsor blaster" (a combination rocket engine and laser beam) capable of making objects seem to explode (temporarily fall apart) at a distance. The repulsor blaster contained a high-performance media computer, Bluetooth, sound system, position sensors, and haptic motors to create a sense of physical impact and an ability to communicate with smart phones and the internet (where kids could download new play experiences).

Long-time Disney licensee Hasbro agreed to make and sell the new line of toys, and the first repulsor blaster hit retail toy shelves in November 2015, just in time for Christmas shopping.

Disney Playmation digital toys will turn kids into Marvel superheroes

The revolutionary play system garnered critical acclaim from journalists who tried it, and multiple awards, including the Parent's Choice Award for 2015 and the 2015 Gold Star Toy award from Scholastic's *Parent & Child* magazine. *Time Magazine* named it a Top-10 Toy of 2015.

But features such as interactive audio and an ability to "destroy" physical objects at a distance that made Playmation so innovative also created major challenges for marketing and advertising. Playmation did so many things that no toy had ever done before that parents shopping in the toy aisle weren't completely sure what made the new toy better than less expensive toys that outwardly looked similar. So Playmation sales were lackluster.

But to Disney, Playmation's disappointing results did not mean that Bob Chapek's original vision for virtual play was wrong. It only meant that, as with many previous ground-breaking innovations, Disney had to keep looking for the right mix of product and market.

So Mike asked the creative and technical team that he led to apply lessons learned from Playmation to alternative ways to marry virtual and physical experiences. But Mike insisted on retaining one key feature of Playmation: encouraging kids to move around vigorously during play.

Hoping to get marketing lift from a planned Lucasfilm movie, Mike's team shifted from Marvel to the Star Wars franchise. A few months into the Star Wars effort, Mike's team made two key discoveries.

Two discoveries

The first discovery stemmed from a prank on Mike's creative lead.

Haseltine, who'd gotten Playmation started with a fairy dollhouse, had been tinkering — in his garage — with new designs for Mike's team. He was working on a head-mounted augmented reality (AR) display system which could essentially project holographic imagery for individual users into any environment.

Mike — who'd never lost his passion for virtual reality (VR) — thought that VR's close cousin, AR (augmented reality), could create novel experiences that married virtual and physical worlds to let kids move around safely (unlike VR, AR lets users see their environment along with virtual imagery).

But to develop AR experiences, Mike needed an AR head-mounted display system to use. While tech giants like Google and Microsoft, and well-funded Magic Leap, had staked out strong positions in the AR display space and would eventually bring AR displays to market that Disney could use, none were available yet. So Mike had a brief chat with Haseltine and encouraged him to slap together a simple prototype that developers could start work on.

A day later the contractor brought in a very crude prototype of a head-mounted augmented reality display system consisting of carved up magnifying lenses and a plastic beam-splitter mirror held together with hot glue and duct tape. Mike, and his lead creative designer, Logan Olson, thought the slap-dash prototype might be eventually be useful, but asked that it be made more compact.

Thus began a cycle that continued over a couple of months, where each day Haseltine would bring from home an AR display prototype that addressed Logan's last objections, only to have Logan say, "Cool, but could you [fix problem A, B, or C]?"

After Haseltine developed and demonstrated 50 different versions (all held together with hot glue and duct tape), Logan said with exasperation, "I don't know.

They're all just too big and clunky. You sure you can't make it smaller?"

Original AR display prototype

As a reductio-ad-absurdum joke, Haseltine immediately went to a work bench in the lab and took 10 minutes to slap together a sub-miniature "derringer" version of the AR display. Then, wearing a look-how-dumb-your request-was smirk, he plopped it on Logan's desk. "There," Haseltine pronounced triumphantly. "Smaller size, but also smaller exit pupil, smaller eye-relief, and smaller field of view; in other words, smaller *everything* you said you couldn't live without."

Logan picked up the in-your-face-insult prototype and looked through it, a wide grin spreading on his face. "This is it!!! Exactly what I want!"

Haseltine frowned. "You're shitting me, right?"

"No." Logan came back. "Now build a more rugged one for me to start developing the new experience."

Haseltine stared at Logan, speechless.

The "derringer"

"Well," Logan asked, "What are you waiting for? You've got a hot glue gun and the rest of the day to build me one I can actually use."

When Haseltine told Mike Goslin that Logan, who was a stickler for pushing the limits to achieve "Disney quality," had finally agreed that he had a prototype with which to start play testing with kids and parents, Mike asked to see the "derringer." Haseltine handed it to him, and Mike looked through the device at a virtual Frozen character, Olaf, standing on a real bench in the Playmation development lab.

Handing the display back to Haseltine, Mike asked, "Is there anything else on the market that does what this does?"

"Not with this wide field of view, not at this price point," Haseltine answered.

"Well," Mike mused, "We never meant to invent and use our own AR display, but it looks like you and Logan just backed into it."

The second discovery occurred during play testing of a high-tech lightsaber with kids and their parents. Like the Iron Man repulsor blaster, the novel lightsaber was networked to other toys and accessories and could move and affect objects at a distance. During the debrief after play testing the lightsaber and accessories, Mike would ask both parents and kids what they thought of the new concept. One father answered, "Well, it's OK, but you know what I really want?"

"What?" Mike asked.

"A *real* lightsaber. You know, with a *real laser beam* leaping from the hilt instead of a lit-up plastic tube."

Mike was about to say that the laws of physics didn't allow laser beams to simply stop in midair, but checked himself as an idea crept into his head.

What if we used the AR display that Logan and Haseltine were tinkering with to holographically project a laser blade onto a moving lightsaber hilt? That would look and feel exactly like the "real" thing in the Star Wars movie.

With this thought fresh in his brain, Mike told the

father, "Thanks for the suggestion. We'll see what we can do about it."

That day, Mike asked Logan and his team to start working on an AR lightsaber experience.

Solving a sticky problem

As work on the AR lightsaber progressed over the next few weeks, a major obstacle emerged: how to get a lightsaber laser image in the AR display to superimpose upon, and precisely track, a fast-moving hilt in the hands of a user. Microsoft had solved this thorny problem with their new Hololens AR system, but Microsoft's solution required far more sensors and computing power than the Disney target price point (less than $200) would allow.

Blue laser blade (right) "sticks" to hilt as player battles villain Kylo Ren

Getting virtual images displayed in an AR headset to "stick" to real world objects, such as lightsaber hilts, had come to be known in AR circles as "the sticking problem." Logan Olson, who had strong technology chops in addition to being a top game designer and creative talent, began to look around for affordable ways to solve it.

Logan's quest led him to a Chinese company called Ximmerse, who had developed a compact, low-cost, two-camera machine vision system that tracked head motion and physical objects in real time, allowing graphics software and hardware in the AR headset to generate virtual images that "stuck" to the physical environment.

Based on Logan's favorable report on Ximmerse, Mike Goslin met with Ximmerse CEO Davey He at a bar in San Francisco while they were both attending the Game Developer's Conference. Mike's goal for the initial meeting was to persuade Ximmerse to see if they could meet Disney's demanding technical requirements and affordable price-point. As with previous business discussions on the project, Mike expected that if he were successful in getting Ximmerse interested, a long series of follow up meetings and negotiations would ensue before a deal could be struck.

But that's not what happened over beers at the San Francisco bar. After Mike explained Disney's vision for virtual/physical active play using AR, Davey thought for a moment and said, "OK, I'm going to do this."

Mike took a long pull on his beer while he collected his thoughts. "You mean you're in for our BOM (bill of material), ceilings, and performance goals?"

Davey smiled. "Yes, I'm in."

And Davey was as good as his word. Within a few weeks, engineers in Mike's group worked with Ximmerse engineers to integrate the Ximmerse computer vision system into the "derringer" display system that Haseltine had developed, and a fully functional, very low-cost AR system was born.

Disney named the new creation "Mirage," which Lenovo ultimately adopted.

Sealing the deal with Lenovo

The first working version of Mirage, with Ximmerse technology, had just been completed when Mike saw Carter Agar in the Disney quad. Mike told Carter he had something to show him.

In my office before the Mirage demo, a few months after we bumped into each other, Carter was skeptical that we could have developed an AR system that did as much as I claimed it did, and cost so little. But when I put the system on him in the lab and let him experience it, he was blown away.

Getting Lenovo on board was important because Disney typically did not manufacture and sell technology. Instead, they simply licensed their intellectual property to others, such as Hasbro and Mattel, to manufacture, market, and sell. In the case of Mirage, Disney needed a technology company to whom they could also license their Mirage optics and other embedded technologies.

Back in China, Carter told his superiors about Mirage and suggested that key Lenovo executives see a demo at the upcoming Consumer Electronics Show (CES) in Las Vegas.

Leading the Lenovo group to see the demo in a private room at an Italian restaurant at the Venetian hotel was Jason Huang, head of manufacturing for the company.

"And at dinner," Mike later said, "right there on the spot, without any further discussion, or any follow up meetings at all, Jason committed Lenovo to manufacture, promote, and sell Mirage. Although we later met with Jason's boss, Jeff Meredith, in Beijing for his approval, essentially the deal had been sealed in the restaurant at CES."

Ten months later, Star Wars™: Jedi Challenges featuring Mirage hit the shelves at Best Buy.

Take-away lessons for innovation

In all, Mirage made it from the first crude, hot-glued prototype to Best Buy in just under 24 months, far less time than it took Microsoft and Magic Leap to get Hololens and Magic Leap AR to market, respectively. And the Lenovo/Disney system cost less than one-tenth those offered by Microsoft and Magic Leap. Although Disney does not reveal how much they spent developing Star Wars™: Jedi Challenges, it's safe to say that their total investment had many fewer zeros behind it than Micro-soft and Magic Leap's investments.

So with Star Wars™: Jedi Challenges, Mike Gos-lin and Disney were able to implement Bob Chapek's original vision of virtual/physical play through faster, better, and more affordable innovation.

And the way Disney pulled it off underscores our main point: innovation happens faster, better, and cheaper when informality and personal relationships dominate the innovation process.

Re-winding and replaying the Star Wars™: Jedi Challenges story, here are the key points that make this case:

- In showing Bob Iger future business opportun-ities, Kevin Mayer used Haseltine, a part-time contractor who slapped prototypes together in a garage instead of an orthodox design and de-velopment lab.

- Bob Chapek decided to green-light the virtual/ physical project without formal "numbers" exercises, based only on the fit of Haseltine's idea with sweeping trends that he envisioned, along with a gut feel that Haseltine represented the kind of culture Disney needed to succeed in the emerging market for virtual play.

- The leader of the Jedi Challenges/Mirage development team, Mike Goslin, from his childhood onward, was not a big fan of rules and formal processes, preferring instead more relaxed methods that emphasized personal relationships.

- This penchant led Mike to nurture a long-term, personal, informal relationship with Lenovo's Carter Agar, a relationship that was based on mutual respect and trust. So, after the two had a chance encounter, collaborating on a new project felt natural to both men.

- Mirage itself emerged not from a formal cascade development process (requirements, design specifications, etc.) but by a quick and scrappy prototyping team that backed into the solution.

- Like Chapek, Davey He of Ximmerse didn't need a detailed, formal business plan to commit his company. Instead, over a beer in a bar, after meeting Mike Goslin only once — and liking what he saw — Davey made an on-the-spot decision.

- Ditto for Lenovo executive Jason, who committed his company — over pasta in Las Vegas — without going through all the usual formalities.

To us, the most encouraging lesson to emerge from the Jedi Challenges saga was that even a massively successful, conservative megalith like Disney can act like an agile start-up when they rely less on numbers in early stages of innovating, and more on relationships, garage-shop development methods, and gut intuition.

In accomplishing this, Mike Goslin and his team were able to quickly harness the monster power of both the Star Wars brand and its marketing juggernaut parent, the Walt Disney Company.

Chapter 4:
Cultivate the right monsters
(before jumping on their backs)

Intelligence failures

Opana Radar Station, Oahu, Hawaii
December 7, 1941

The two lowly Army privates did their job, exactly as ordered, but as often is the case — in the eyes of enlisted men, anyhow — it was an *officer* who screwed things up.

Privates Joe Lockard, from Harrisburg, PA, and George Elliot, from Chicago, IL, had volunteered to operate the brand spanking new SCR 270 B radar, one of six such systems recently installed to scan the sky for enemy planes around the Hawaiian Islands.

Although tensions with the Japanese were high, Hawaii military installations were not on a particularly high level of alert, so around 7:00 AM, George Elliot was just fiddling around with the new radar, getting used to it, when he spotted a bright light that looked to him, and to Lockard, like about 50 planes.

The privates called in the sighting to the Fort Shafter

Information Center in Honolulu. A Lt. Kermit Tyler took the call, thought about it briefly, then told the two privates not to worry about the blips because they were probably just a group of American B-17 bombers.

It turns out that Lt. Taylor was wrong, because about 40 minutes later, Japanese bombers, the true source of the radar sighting, attacked Pearl Harbor, killing 2,403 Americans and pulling the US into World War II.

Over the years, the US Intelligence Community has taken steps to ensure that another Pearl Harbor never again catches America by surprise. For example, the Central Intelligence Agency was established 6 years after Pearl Harbor. Central in its name signified it was the place into which all the dots would flow and then be connected through a process called "All-source" analysis.

But repeated major surprises cropped up after Pearl Harbor, such as India's first nuclear test in May 1974, and then of course, 9/11.

Despite concerted efforts to close intelligence blind spots immediately after 9/11, another massive intelligence failure — the assessments of weapons of mass destruction in Iraq that justified the invasion — occurred less than 18 months after 9/11.

Most recently, something akin to a cyber Pearl Harbor stealthily compromised numerous sensitive government networks, including some related to management of nuclear weapons. The attack went undetected for many months, requiring a tip-off not from the intelligence agencies, FBI or Department of Homeland Security, but from a private cyber security company called FireEye.

What to do about it

Job number one for the US Intelligence Community is to prevent surprise. But it is understandable that they haven't always done this well because preventing surprises requires accurate prediction, and as Nobel Prize winner Niels Bohr said, "Prediction is difficult: especially of the future."

In Chapter 2, we told the story of how DARPA spawned the Internet. DARPA has also fostered other military game-changers such as spy satellites, stealth aircraft, and Predator drones. And all of these DARPA advances, curiously enough, came out of President Eisenhower's desire to prevent another technological surprise like Russia's 1957 launch of Sputnik.

So, does the US Intelligence Community, which is all about preventing surprise, have its own version of DARPA?

Yes, it does: IARPA (Intelligence Advanced Research Projects Activity). And IARPA has actually put a dent in the ever-present prediction problem, sometimes improving upon the track record of even the most experienced and skilled intelligence analysts.

One of the IARPA projects aimed at improving prediction accuracy, as you might expect from a government agency, had a title that conveyed very little information about what the project actually did.

The project was called Aggregative Contingent Estimation, or ACE for short, and was kicked off about a decade ago. It adopted an approach called "artificial Artificial Intelligence," meaning ACE fostered creation of a system whereby a group of talented humans mimicked the performance of an ultra-advanced AI, if only that AI existed.[1]

In other words, despite IARPA being all about technology, especially digital technology, ACE sought to exploit human neurons sitting in living, human brains more than integrated circuits sitting in computers.

IARPA's approach to predicting the future, spearheaded by University of Pennsylvania's Philip Tetlock, systematically identified superforecasters. These people have a natural gift for prediction. IARPA then trains these forecasters and supplies them with tools to improve their access to information and thus, accuracy of predictions.

The IARPA project has also developed algorithms for combining the predictions of multiple superforcasters into a single, more accurate composite prediction.[2]

Notable successes of IARPA-sponsored superforcasting, or offshoots of IARPA programs, include[3]:

- accurate prediction the UK would approve a Brexit deal in 2020

- the decision in 2019 of Saudi Arabia to take its national gas company public

- developments in Russia's food embargo against certain European countries in 2019

- other developments we can't talk about, but trust us, you would be impressed if you learned about them

The bottom line here is that IARPA, although only created in 2008, is well on its way to helping the Intelligence Community do job number one better.

All well and good. But what does any of this have to do with the main theme of this book: emphasizing the importance of informality and personal relationships in fostering big breakthroughs in big bureaucracies?

The answer to that question is that IARPA itself—and all the good work it has done—is the product of highly informal, highly personal interactions among a few people who respected and trusted each other. This proves that there's hope even for big government bureaucracies such as the US Intelligence Community.

We say this with some authority because one of the authors of this book, together with his deputy Steve Nixon, actually *created* IARPA in the first place.

Therefore, what follows is more or less a firsthand account, with major contributions from "co-conspirators" such as Steve Nixon, Maryland Representative

Dutch Ruppersberger, and most importantly, the mother of all DC cockroaches, one Gary L. Sojka.

Mr. Cockroach

Although one author believes that he and Steve Nixon deserve most of the credit (and all of the blame) for creating IARPA, that's not really true. The lion's share of the credit goes to Gary Sojka, one of the founding members of an informal organization of current and former intelligence/national security professionals, simply called ... the Cockroaches.

Gary's story, including the founding of the Cockroaches, is worth diving into here, because it illustrates the point we are trying to make: that informal, personal relationships are vital to innovation. Near the end of Gary's story, we'll explain how he catalyzed IARPA's creation.

But let's first take a close look at Gary himself.

Gary grew up in a working-class family as an only child in Buffalo, New York, and Williamsport, Pennsylvania. Despite having loving parents, the lack of siblings left Gary feeling lonely, isolated, lacking social skills developed from the normal give and take with brothers and sisters. He had a large extended family, which he felt part of while in Buffalo, but his ability to connect with that family disappeared when he moved to Williamsport.

Because of his perceived lack of social skills, in high school, Gary felt isolated and belonged to no cliques.

"I felt insecure about the number of friends that I had, I didn't feel like I had family connections, and I lacked the skills to make people interested in me or to like me" Gary said.

Gary thinks that his early sense of isolation motivated him to become an ardent networker once he became a Washington, DC, fixture. With each new networking group he set up, or helped set up, his goal was the same: to form groups "rich in warmth and humanity," the kind of warmth and humanity he seldom got from belonging to groups as a child.

Anyone with even a passing familiarity with Washington, DC, might suspect warmth and humanity are oxymoronic with Washington and DC, but, astoundingly, Gary and his like-minded associates have pulled it off not once, but multiple times.

Gary's career, moving from one government organization to another, making connections along the way, helped him form the nucleus of many of the networking groups that he would later organize.

One of his first jobs was working in Naval Intelligence on attack submarine missions. From there, he moved to the Defense Intelligence Agency (DIA) where he led a branch of analysts studying Strategic Force Operations (i.e., nuclear weapons and nuclear war). Later, Gary helped CIA analyst Dr. Larry Gershwin develop a report titled National Intelligence Estimates of Adversaries' Science and Technology.

Eventually, Gary left the executive branch of government for the legislative branch, becoming a staffer on the Senate Select Committee on Intelligence and Senate Armed Services Committee, where he got deeply involved in helping Congress decide which intelligence technology projects to fund, at what level of funding.

Today, Gary is in the "advocacy" business, which is another way of saying he is a lobbyist. He works with tech companies who offer products and services for national security, specializing in helping them navigate the byzantine maze that is DC.

Although lobbyist is a dirty word in some quarters—with some justification—the reality is that not all lobbyists are bad, and not everything lobbyists accomplish is swamp-like.

What Gary, in particular, does as a lobbyist, is to bridge the divides that prevent technology from making its way out of R&D labs into the hands of soldiers and intelligence officers who need it.

One of these divides is with smallish technology companies who haven't a clue how to do business with the government. Yet here is where some of the most innovative, breakthrough technologies emerge (like Predator drones). Gary helps bridge that divide.

Before he became a lobbyist and was still working in the government, Gary discovered a vast divide between scientists and engineers in R&D labs everywhere—whether in industry or government—and the ultimate end-users of R&D technology. R&D geeks and the people who fund the transition of R&D technology into production frequently don't like or respect each other very much, creating relationship deficits that inhibit adoption of innovative technologies.

The reason, Gary knows, is a universal truism about human nature: people don't buy products from organizations, they buy them from *people* (and in this case, we're talking about *people* adopting promising R&D innovations from *people*). People they like. People they respect. And, above all, people they *trust*.

The trouble is, R&D types are often introverted and sometimes arrogant and dismissive of "short-sighted" mere mortals without advanced degrees, or, shudder, gasp, *no degrees whatsoever!* And unfortunately for R&D labs, another name for mere mortals without advanced degrees is ... customers of R&D innovation, such as fighter pilots, intelligence analysts, and procurement officials who buy technology for fighter pilots and intelligence analysts.

On the flip side, procurement officials, military types, and intelligence officers who could benefit from R&D innovations frequently perceive R&D professionals to be clueless geeks who talk down to them, *if* they stoop low enough to talk to them *at all*. "Mental masturbators" is a term oft heard in the same sentence as R&D scientists, along with "ivory tower egg-heads," or simply, "arrogant jerks."

Passionate about new technology's promise to solve vexing national security challenges (such as knowing where adversary forces are at all times), Gary thought long and hard about how to get innovations to leap over the valley of death that separates R&D innovators, and their ingrained culture, from R&D customers, and *their* deeply ingrained, diametrically opposed, culture.

Being street smart after so many years in the belly of beast of DC, Gary knew the answer to this pervasive problem wasn't to be found in any bureaucratic policy, procedure, document, or anything that in any way resembled a formal process. The answer lay in getting human beings in R&D labs and human beings in the operational world to somehow view each other as the human beings they actually were.

In short, what was called for to bridge the valley of death was ... good food washed down by decent booze, consumed as far away as possible from sterile, oppressive government buildings.

In pursuit of this social engineering project, Gary became a serial networking entrepreneur. Along with Mike Swetnam, Charlie Scalera, and Tim Sample, he set up the Potomac Institute for Policy Studies (PIPS). With Dr. Robert Hummel, he set up United States Technology Leadership Council (USTLC). At the request of George Spahe, he helped set up the Advanced Intelligence Technology Association. He provided support to Steve Jacques and John Stopher as they set up the US GeoSpatial Intelligence Foundation (USGIF) and the Advanced Technology Intelligence Association (ATIA). He provided similar support to Rich Coleman as he set up the Cyber, Space, and Intelligence Association

(CSIA). But finally, and most importantly, he and Mike Swetnam created an iconic group in Washington, DC— The Cockroaches.

The goal of each of these informal groups was the same: bring mid-level government types together with each other, throwing mid-level technology types from industry into the mix, with liberal application of quality food, quality alcohol, and resulting quality conversations. And of course, to draw people to meetings with marquee speakers such as congressmen, senators and cabinet-level officials.

Cockroaches founders Gary Sojka (L) and Charlie Scalera (R) at early Cockroaches dinner

Perhaps an even bigger draw to Gary's many meetings was the feeling of family that he scrupulously cultivated, stressing informality, good-natured ribbing, jokes, and lots of "you-should-have-been-there war stories. With these gatherings, Gary created an extended family of "brothers and sisters" that he missed growing up.

Gary focused on recruiting mid-level leaders because "those usually are the people who actually make the key decisions and get things done." The people Gary recruited into these groups were also often those who occupied a much higher place on an *unofficial* org chart than they did on any *official* org chart, because again, "those are the people who really get things done." In the first chapter, we met one of these stealthy, but shockingly powerful and effective innovation leaders, Brian Hibbeln.

The Cockroaches gets its name from the idea that only cockroaches survive radiation exposure in nuclear wars, and in DC, workers below cabinet-level, who aren't political appointees, survive when all those above them get "nuked" with the swearing in of a new president.

Full disclosure, Haseltine has been a card-carrying cockroach, complete with cockroach tie pin (see below) and is, in the interest of full transparency, also currently the Chairman of the Board of the Sojka-founded US Technology Leadership Council. Which is another way of saying that we are not objective about Gary and his accomplishments because he, along with his wife Gwen, are friends.

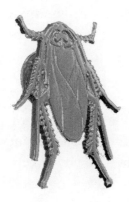

Official cockroach membership pin

Gary's wife Gwen, by the way, is an enormously important part of Gary's success getting things done through relationship building over good food and good conversations. For instance, Gwen not only is in charge of day-to-day operations of the US Technology Leadership Council, but also ensures that the meals at frequent dinner meetings rival those of great restaurants.

The importance of good food cannot be overstated because, as DC veteran, Steve Nixon, whom you'll meet shortly, observed, "All of Gary's meetings are voluntary, so if you want people to come, you'd better have something really compelling to draw them in."

Gwen herself, warm, friendly to a fault, and a great listener (a truly rare thing in DC) — as much as the marquee speakers — is another big draw to Gary's events.

One of the most notable and important products of Gary's informal, relationship-based approach, pulled off with the aid of fellow Cockroaches, Congressman Dutch Ruppersberger and Steve Nixon, was the creation of IARPA.

The real story of IARPA's creation

Like most organizations with a concrete, here-and-now mission, the US Intelligence Community, especially after 9/11, Iraq, and Afghanistan, was too busy with day-to-day operations to waste much time thinking about the future.

Thus, for decades, improvements to technologies that collected intelligence (e.g., satellites) and analyzed intelligence (e.g., IT systems) advanced at a slow, incremental pace through evolutionary steps versus revolutionary leaps. Wasting time on pie-in-the-sky breakthrough inventions was deemed too great a risk to mission. So intelligence agencies almost without exception would tweak, extend, expand, and upgrade existing technology rather than invest in completely new technology. Virtually all funding for intelligence tech went to massive "programs for the record" that had been around for decades, and would be around for decades to come, which sucked all the money, and life, away from fledgling new developments.

Thus, when the Office of the Director of National Intelligence (ODNI) formed in 2005, Haseltine, its first Director of Science and Technology, along with his deputy, Steve Nixon, set as their primary goal increasing emphasis on high-risk, high-reward intelligence R&D.

What Haseltine and his deputy wanted was an Intelligence version of DARPA.

Haseltine and his deputy, Steve Nixon, who had worked in the Navy and as a Congressional staffer, both knew that the task would be formidable because "increasing emphasis on high-risk high-reward technologies" was a polite way of saying, "we are going to steal money away from the evolutionary in order to fund the revolutionary."

The challenge, of course, is that individuals who had possession of the money ODNI coveted for this endeavor were very fond of their money, as were members of Congress who, for their own reasons, funded incremental technology programs in the different agencies, particularly in the CIA. Since 1947, as the leader of the entire Intelligence Community, the CIA had the responsibility to develop technologies that benefited multiple agencies. Every fiscal year, they got funding aimed not at advancing the CIA's sole mission (collection of Human Intelligence and All Source Analysis), but at advancing missions that cut across multiple agencies, such as space-based surveillance.

All that changed when Congress shifted responsibility for cross-agency R&D from the CIA to ODNI in 2005. At that time, CIA did not agree with ODNI that cross-agency R&D efforts, and above all the funding for those efforts, should move from the CIA to ODNI. After all, CIA asserted, "We are still the CENTRAL Intelligence Agency."

What followed was a bureaucratic DC food fight of epic proportions that got really down and dirty. CIA made overtures to an ODNI staffer working for Haseltine and Steve, perhaps, as the CIA is known to do, to gain "Human Intelligence" on ODNI's plans. And on two different occasions, the CIA pushed to get the Director himself fired.

The fight for money in Congress was equally brutal, with one member in particular, a long-time CIA ally, putting up major resistance to ODNI's efforts to move money from the CIA to ODNI for its own DARPA. That member, who occupied a seat on the House Permanent Select Committee on Intelligence (HPSCI) asked for voluminous, detailed plans, only to reject plan after plan as "insufficient."

After one especially fractious meeting with that member on Capitol Hill, Haseltine and Steve retreated to their offices on Bolling Air Force Base to regroup.

"She [the member] is never going to let HPSCI authorize the fund transfer," Haseltine observed, nursing his 9th Diet Coke that day. "We can come up with new plans and answer her objections till the cows come home, but the answer will always be the same: NO."

"Yep," Steve simply said, as the two lapsed into thoughtful silence.

At length, Steve looked up, the scowl on his face relaxing. "Got an idea that just might, might work."

Haseltine, who had grown bone-weary of the struggle that had twice nearly gotten him fired, and who wasn't optimistic that anything new would work, launched his empty soda can into a nearby trash container, and answered his deputy with only a long, mournful sigh. Uncharacteristically, Haseltine left without saying another word.

But Steve, who'd survived many a bureaucratic DC knife fight — and won most of them — wasn't so pessimistic, because he knew Gary Sojka.

So, Luke Skywalker (Steve) sought wise counsel from Yoda (Gary) on how to get through, over, or around the formidable obstacles standing in IARPA's way. This sort of conversation was, after all, what the Cockroaches were all about.

Gary and his partner, Charlie Scalera, met with Steve over dinner. Integral to the strategy to get IARPA going was to ensure that the Senate Select Committee on Intelligence (SSCI) was in favor of the creation of IARPA. Gary and Charlie had a number of friends — Cockroaches — on the SSCI's Technical Advisory Group, including Mike Swetnam and Greg Poe. Moreover, Gary was close to Ken Johnson — another Cockroach — who was the professional staffer on the committee working for Maryland Senator Barbara Milkulski. Ken and Gary had worked together for years when Gary was a professional staffer. When leadership changes on the Senate Armed Services Committee resulted in personnel changes on that staff, Gary was instrumental in helping Ken land a position on the SSCI. Along with Senator Mikulski's role on the SSCI, Senator Mikulski was a senior member of the powerful Senate Appropriations Committee and Dean of the Maryland Delegation. Gary and Charlie worked closely to enlist the support of the SSCI TAG and Senator Mikulski.

Another piece integral to the strategy was to run this by Congressman Ruppersberger, nicknamed Dutch. Gary had gotten to know Congressman Ruppersberger through his partner Charlie. When Dutch was elected to Congress and was appointed to the HPSCI, Charlie arranged for him to meet Gary over dinner at the iconic Capitol Hill restaurant, The Monocle. Gary, at the time, was acting as the DC-fundraiser for then HPSCI Chairman, Pete Hoekstra. Hoekstra was a Republican and Dutch was a Democrat, who had strong bipartisan credentials. Charlie wanted Dutch to get to know the Chairman to ensure Dutch could work with the other side of the aisle. Gary told Pete that he could work with Dutch and arranged for the two to meet socially to get to know each other.

To help Dutch get to know the intelligence community better, Gary and Mike Swetnam, co-chairs of the Cockroaches, made Dutch a Cockroach, and invited him to speak to gain recognition.

Next came the third part of the strategic coalition. Charlie was a close friend with the then President of the University of Maryland, Daniel Mote. Charlie and Gary went to meet with Mote to suggest that he support the creation of IARPA and that he offer the University of Maryland campus as a location. The university was already strongly involved in providing technical support to US Intelligence. Mote agreed. He further agreed, when given the signal by Charlie and Gary, to call the Maryland Congressional delegation and urge their support of the creation of IARPA and offer his campus as a location.

With Mote's support locked up, Charlie and Gary arranged for a dinner with Dutch and Steve at The Capital Grille.

After 9/11, Dutch was one of 8 members of Congress who pushed for the creation of ODNI in the first place, out of belief that the existing structure of the Intelligence Community, where communication and coordination were less than perfect, was not up to the task of preventing additional 9/11 type-surprises.

Partly as a result of long conversations with Gary, Dutch also grew convinced that the Intelligence Community needed a lot more "out of the box thinking" and technology, like that provided to the Military by DARPA. And Dutch agreed with Gary that any DARPA-like organization should live at ODNI, which would not feel the constant pull of day-to-day intelligence operations that would remorselessly push long-term projects to have shorter and shorter-term objectives.

So when Gary mentioned to Dutch the difficulties Steve was encountering, Dutch was sympathetic and said he'd be open to meeting with Steve and Gary over dinner.

During the meal near the Capitol building, Steve

laid out the rationale for IARPA along with the road-blocks preventing its formation.

Armed with that information, Dutch, who was Chairman of the Technical and Tactical sub-committee, worked with his staff to do a cost-benefit analysis of how and where an Intelligence DARPA should be formed.

When the analysis clearly showed that the most cost-effective solution was to house any DARPA-like activity near a university in the DC metropolitan area, the University of Maryland was ready to step up and make it known to the delegation with calls by Mote to every member and senator. The University already housed Intelligence research groups such as NSA's Disruptive Technology Office and University of Maryland's Center for Advanced Study of Language; Dutch called Maryland Senator Barb Mikulski to explore ways to make an Intelligence DARPA a reality.

Shortly after that conversation, Haseltine took a call at his brother's house in Georgetown, where he often stayed while working in DC. The call went something like this:

"Eric, Barb Mikulski."

"It's a great honor, Senator. To what do I owe the pleasure of this call?"

"Word has reached my ears that you are considering concentrating all ODNI R&D work in Northern Virginia, moving centers out of the University of Maryland."

"That's true, Senator. We don't have the money to do otherwise because we can't get IARPA stood up."

There was a brief pause. "So your problem is money. Do you know how much you need and what you'll do with it?"

"Oh, yes [insert name of HPSCI member who had been fighting tooth and nail against IARPA] has really made us do our homework, down to the last particular. We have a very detailed budget and schedule."

"Ok, expect a call from Steny."

Haseltine hung up, poured himself a large glass of his brother's most expensive whisky, and swallowed it quickly, then added ice and refilled his glass.

"Whoa," he thought. "I wonder if that's what Steve [Nixon] set in motion. I seldom get calls from sitting senators. Hell, I NEVER get those calls. That's impressive. And Steny, no less, will call me too. WOW!"

In the middle of that thought the phone rang again. "Eric, Steny" (as, in House Majority Leader Steny Hoyer.)

"Majority Leader, great to hear from you."

"Barb says you need some money. What do you need it for, exactly?"

"Well, sir, we need a new building, new principal investigators and staff, and more dollars to fund academic and government research lab."

"Ok, what are we talking about."

"Sir?"

"How much *money* do you need, Eric?"

"Oh." Haseltine gave the House Majority leader a number.

"Is that all? All this fuss was only about THAT?"

"Yes, sir."

"And you'll keep the work in Maryland." It was a statement, not a question.

"Yes, sir."

"Ok, I think we can help you out."

For those not up to speed on the ways of DC, when the House Majority Leader tells you he can help you out: touchdown, game over, you have won and can do a victory dance in the end-zone.

But even when you've won in Washington, DC, your job is far from over, because literally thousands of details still need to be worked out, the federal bureaucracy being what it is.

Even after Steny Hoyer had determined IARPA was going to happen, resistance among members of the HPSCI (who theoretically authorized Intelligence funding) lingered, so it ultimately was left to the House Appropriations Committee (HAC) of Congress to actually set aside money to make IARPA a reality. At a decisive hearing chaired by Rush Holt, when the Holt was weighing all of the arguments for and against IARPA, he turned to committee staffer Josh Hartman and asked, "Should we do this?"

Josh, who was a friend of Steve Nixon's (having taken Steve's job when Steve moved to ODNI), simply said, "Yes."

"After that," Steve Nixon later said, "the deal was done despite simmering resistance from HPSCI."

And the rest, as they say, is history. With one interesting footnote.

After Congress, with Dutch, Steny, Barb, and Rush Holt leading the way signaled that an Intelligence DARPA was going to be funded, Haseltine and Steve asked for and were granted an audience with the new Director of National Intelligence, Admiral Mike Mc-Connell. The S&T Director and Steve needed to brief him on developments and give him a heads-up that a big congressional "plus up" for the future budget was likely coming.

Admiral McConnell, who had once run NSA, liked everything about an Intelligence DARPA, and only had one question.

"What do you propose to call this new entity?"

"IARPA," Haseltine replied.

The Admiral frowned. "IARPA," he repeated, working hard to get his lips to form around too many vowels in a row. "No," he said, "that won't fly. We are never, ever going to call it something so dorky."

Steve and Haseltine exchanged nervous glances, because IARPA was the name they had sold to Congress, and Congress was the one that wrote all the checks.

Steve said, "Yes, sir, we'll come up with a better name."

And although Admiral McConnell left office at the end of George W. Bush's term (he was a political appointee that got "nuked" by yet another administration change), we expect he is still waiting for IARPA to get its permanent name.

DC being the way it is, he may have a while to wait.

References

1. "Aggregate Contingent Estimation (ACE)," *Office of the Director of National Intelligence, IARPA* (website), accessed April 20, 2020, https://www.iarpa.gov/index.php/research-programs/ace

2. "Philip Tetlock: A Short Course in Superforecasting," *Office of the Director of National Intelligence, IARPA* (website), accessed April 20, 2020, https://www.iarpa.gov/index.php/newsroom/iarpa-in-the-news/2015/556-philip-tetlock-a-short-course-in-superforecasting

3. Tara Law, "'Superforecasters' Are Making Eerily Accurate Predictions About COVID-19. Our Leaders Could Learn From Their Approach," *Time* magazine (website), June 11, 2020, https://time.com/5848271/superforecasters-covid-19/

Chapter 5:
Persuade the monster to
do more of what it does best

February, 2004. Route Irish (Highway of Death),
Baghdad area, Iraq

Sitting in the back of an up-armored SUV, Haseltine, a US Government civilian, checked the rivets holding his shoulder holster to its leather straps for the fifth time since putting on his holster, and the Baretta 9mm it held, shortly before breakfast that morning. Haseltine, who was temporarily deployed from the States on a fact-finding mission, had been humiliated and embarrassed on a previous trip downrange to Iraq when a rivet had worked loose, causing the holster and its heavy contents to fall to the ground. Although the weapon had not discharged, the Major General accompanying Haseltine immediately ordered him to get down and do 50 push-ups.

"Maybe that will remind you to check your gear before you try to play soldier again," the General had said. Then he inspected Haseltine's unmarked, somewhat rumpled uniform closely, knelt down and tied the man's military-issue boots correctly. "For better or for worse, you're in my unit here, and my responsibility. Try to look professional, for once, will you?"

Now, two months later, Haseltine was halfway to Baghdad on his daily trip from Camp Victory near the airport to the Green Zone. He was acutely aware that, although he was dressed like them and armed like them, body armor and all, he didn't really fit in with the three Michigan National Guardsmen who were taking him to Baghdad.

The men had not spoken to him since leaving Camp Victory, and Haseltine could almost feel the waves of resentment rising off of them. He imagined they were thinking, "We're risking our lives every day, getting blown to pieces by an IED or an ambush, just to ferry some DC jerk-off back and forth on Route Irish. And for what? Most of these civvy ass-wipes just come here for a day or two for a photo-op so they can go home, look all heroic, and tell war stories that never happened."

Looking at the rigid posture of the Master Sergeant in the passenger seat in front of him, Haseltine thought about ways to connect with the soldiers who clearly didn't want him there. Like everyone, he supposed, he wanted people to like him, but more importantly, his life literally depended on these three. Small arms ambushes along Route Irish were getting more common, and so were IED attacks. And just that morning, in the security brief, he'd learned that insurgents were starting to drop grenades on coalition vehicles from overpasses.

Things could get ugly fast, and the civilian wondered how soldiers, who objected to his very existence,
would keep him alive when the shit started flying.

Getting an idea, he cleared his throat and turned to
the young officer sitting beside him. "Lieutenant, got a
question."

Keeping his eyes out the window, scanning the
area for threats, the officer said in a neutral voice, "OK,
shoot."

"Uh, we've been working stateside on new ways to
counter IEDs, and I wanted to run one of our ideas by
you to see if you think it would help."

Eyes still scanning the surround, the Lieutenant
simply nodded, indicating the civilian should continue.

"Ok, so the tech we are developing, if we can get it
to work, would tell you whenever you were approach-
ing the frag radius [lethal blast zone] of a device. Could
you use that?"

For the first time that morning, the Army officer
turned to face the civilian, locking eyes with him.
Haseltine took note of the Lieutenant's intense green
eyes with flecks of yellow in the irises. "So," the man
asked, "how would it work?"

"Well, I can't go into details, but if it does what we
hope, it will set off an alarm when you get within, say
300 meters of an IED."

"What do you mean, 'If it does what we hope?' Does
it work or not?" Haseltine checked himself, remem-
bering that soldiers in combat had little patience for

anything they couldn't use to stay alive here-and-now, and didn't appreciate wasting time on vapor-ware bullshit.

Nervous, Haseltine pressed on anyhow. "It's in the research stage, in the lab. But I'm here to find out whether or not it will really help if we somehow do manage to make it work—for at least some classes of IEDs. Sometimes, the way things look from DC are not really the way things are here. That's why I've come: to do a reality check."

The officer's features went deadpan. "Why, Doctor, you think geekazoids in lab coats don't understand our problems? Whatever gave you that idea?

Haseltine sighed. "Ok, yeah. I am one of those geekazoids. Guilty as charged. But I've been here a few times now, enough to know that we really don't understand you or your problems. But some of us really do want to try to understand."

The two regarded each other, unblinking. At length the officer's expression softened. "Ok. got it. So you want to know if we'd like some sort of I&W [indications and warning] of an IED ahead."

"That's right."

"Would it tell us exactly where the IED was ahead? Straight? Right? Left?"

"Maybe. But let's suppose it were a simple light with a buzzer that triggered when you approached."

The Lieutenant nodded. "Yeah. We could use that. In fact, it would be great. When can we have it?"

Haseltine was about to answer when he caught
something out of the corner of his eye, a slight adjust-
ment in the posture of the Master Sergeant in the front
seat. The Lieutenant, a Reserve Officer Training Candi-
dacy (ROTC) grad two years out of college and on his
first combat tour, had learned the hard way to pay close
attention to his sergeant, who, nearly 20 years his senior, had been in the shit many times before, including
Grenada and Desert Storm.

"Something to say, Master Sergeant?" The Lieutenant asked.

The sergeant answered, "Permission to speak freely,
SIR!"

The young officer in the back seat rolled his eyes,
favoring the civilian with a see-what-I-have-to-put-up-
with look. He answered, "Go ahead, Master Sergeant."

The senior enlisted man turned in his seat to face
the civilian. "SIR. With all due respect, SIR. That's the
dumbest fucking idea I've ever heard. SIR." With that,
he turned back around, eyes forward.

Haseltine smiled, realizing he was getting somewhere. Growing up on a military base he knew that senior NCOs (Non Commissioned Officers, like sergeants)
were the ones who actually knew the score and had
the best insights about what was smart and what was
dumb. More, if NCOs didn't want to waste time with
you, they'd simply keep their mouths shut, give you a
tight smile, and watch you fuck-up, all by yourself.

But this NCO hadn't done that. He'd done Haseltine the great favor of telling him he didn't know what the fuck he was talking about. That meant there was hope Haseltine might actually learn something from the NCO.

"Ok, Master Sergeant. Why is that the dumbest fucking idea you've ever heard?"

"Simple. If it's like everything else we get like that, the god damned thing will probably go off all the time when it shouldn't, being a royal pain in the ass. But suppose it actually works as advertised. Then, guess what?"

"What?"

"I'll tell you what. We'll have TTP [Tactics Techniques Procedures] to go with the stupid fucking thing, right? We'll have to follow those TTPs. Like, stop outside the frag zone and wait for EOD [Explosive Ordinance Disposal] to show up to neutralize the sucker."

"I suppose," Haseltine said.

"Yeah, you suppose, right. You know what another name for grunts waiting on a highway out here is? Dead grunts because we'll be sitting ducks for the Muj [short for Mujahadeen insurgents]."

"Mm," Haseltine muttered.

"Yeah, and one more thing," the NCO said. "We've killed or captured all the dumb insurgents, so the ones left are smart. Smart enough to watch what we do and daisy chain the real explosive back to where we'll stop."

"Oh"

"Yeah. Oh. You got one thing right, DOCTOR. The way things look from DC aren't the way they are here."

Haseltine collected himself then ventured, "Ok Master Sergeant, what do you recommend?" The NCO turned in his seat with a wide grin. Then he told Haseltine exactly what to do.

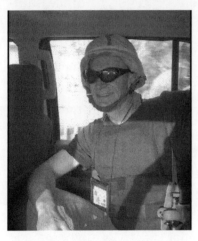

Haseltine in the backseat, the morning he learned his concept was a "dumb fucking idea."

In the Green Zone

A half-hour later, Haseltine went to the communications center in the Green Zone and called a scientist working for him back home. The eight-hour time difference between Iraq and DC meant he would be waking up his subordinate, but in war, new ideas—especially those that can save lives—can't wait.

Haseltine identified himself. "Greg [not his real name], sorry to wake you."

Groggy, Greg said, "No problem. Given where you are, it's probably important."

"It is. Can you get to a grey line [classified phone line at work] in the next hour?"

Greg, yawning, "Sure. Yeah. You got my office number?"

"Yep."

An hour later, Haseltine called the grey line number and Greg picked up on the first ring.

Haseltine told Greg what the Master Sergeant had suggested should be done regarding IEDs that was quite different from the proximity alerting system currently being researched in the lab. Then he asked, "Do you think that can be done?"

Greg cleared his throat. "Oh yes, in fact we just started doing something very much like it elsewhere." He went on to describe the new approach that the lab was testing in another theater of war. [1,2,3,4]

"How long would it take to try the same thing here?"

"Depends how long it would take to task the right asset [piece of equipment] there."

"What kind of asset are we talking about?"

Greg gave him a list of possibilities, which Haseltine jotted down in his notebook. "Thanks. We need to jump on this right away. Can you pull together a team, a budget, and a schedule?"

"Will do."

"And Greg, is there anything I can learn over here that will help you?"

A pause. Then, "Yeah. Can you run over to EOD forensics and get what info you can on the latest and greatest IEDs being scooped up from the battlefield? We need that to work our magic."

"You got it."

A few seconds after Haseltine hung up and was about to start looking for a ride over to EOD to get the information Greg had asked for, an Air Force Major in desert camos approached.

"Doc, you don't know me, but you're something of a celebrity here, being who you are and where you work and all." He extended his hand. "Dakota Willis [not his real name]."

Haseltine shook the officer's hand. "Whatever you've heard about me is lies."

"But Sir, it's all good."

"Then it's *definitely* all lies."

The Major nodded, accepting the banter in stride. Haseltine wasn't military, but he knew how the military talked to one another, and he wanted to blend in, to be accepted.

Major Willis said, "I hope you don't mind, close quarters and all. I overheard your end of the conversation."

Haseltine asked, "You with the '2' [military intelligence]?"

"C2 [Joint Forces Intelligence]. Yes. Why?"

"Well, then, it seems to me it's your job to eaves-drop, especially on pencil-neck civilians, isn't it?"

"Ouch. I'm not a HUMINTER [Human Intelligence Spook], if that's what you mean."

"Relax, Major, I'm just jerking your chain. You wouldn't respect me if I didn't, would you?"

A big smile spread on the Major's face, "Actually, no, I wouldn't. But I think I may be able to help you out."

"Oh?"

"Yes, sir. One of my jobs is to task some of the assets I heard you talking about. I can write up the tasking order if you want. What should it say?"

"Whoa. You mean, just like that, poof, you can order the asset to run test missions for us?"

"Yep. Truth be told, we don't really know what to do with one of them in particular. We've got it, yes, but honestly, it and its crew are just sitting in [location], thumb up their butts, doing diddly squat."

Haseltine opened his notebook, wrote down Greg's grey line number, and tore out the page, then folded the page and handed it to the major. "You got a grey line?"

"Just like you do."

"Ok, call a guy named Greg at this number, tell him I asked you to connect, and ask him to explain exactly what he needs the asset to do."

"Happily."

Haseltine was about to reach for the phone to arrange transport to the EOD cell when Major Willis said, "I can run you over to EOD too, if you want."

Haseltine frowned, "So, you really were eavesdropping, weren't you?"

"You wouldn't respect me if I didn't now, would you?"

Haseltine gave the Major an affectionate pat on the back before strapping on his gear to go back out onto Route Irish on the way to EOD. "I think we're going to get along, Major. I think we understand each other."

The Major came back. "Well, at least I'll make you think we are getting along, won't I?"

Haseltine regarded the major for a moment. "And you say you aren't just another one of those sociopathic, manipulative HUMINTERS, right?"

"That's my story and I'm sticking to it. Now, do you want a lift or not?"

The rest of the story, and what it means

Less than two months later, the asset Major Willis tasked began performing its mission, doing exactly what the Master Sergeant had suggested, significantly cutting down causalities from roadside bombs.

Two months.

The Pentagon can't even order a re-supply of ground coffee in two months, let alone design, develop, and deploy to the battlefield a game-changing, life-saving new technology, such as the one the civilian, Greg, and Major Willis partnered on in Iraq in early 2004.

So just how did the monster bureaucracy to top all monster bureaucracies—the Pentagon—manage to move an innovation out of the lab and onto the battle-field in two short months?

The answer can be found in the two conversations that began this chapter, one in an up-armored SUV, and one in the Green Zone.

The content of the conversations themselves is less important than the context and tone of the conversations.

The context of the conversations was that they took place in settings that were not formally meant to address the challenge of IEDs. No power point slides, no executive summaries, no budgets, no schedules, no buzz words, no ego-stroking or any of the other trappings of a bureaucracy. Just straight ahead, simple discussions among humans who find themselves thrown together in a stressful situation.

We believe that the reason the Master Sergeant gave Haseltine the greatest gift any NCO has to offer—the truth—was not so much due to anything Haseltine said that morning, but to his simple presence on Route Irish. Dignitaries visiting Iraq just for photo-ops and pseudo war stories invariably stayed inside the wire (barbed wired perimeter of a secure base) where the risks of getting killed were relatively low.

But Route Irish was something else entirely. It had gotten the moniker Highway of Death for a very good reason. At that time, the road connecting the Baghdad airport to the city center was the most heavily attacked target in Iraq. On later visits Haseltine made to Iraq, things on Route Irish had gotten so bad the military prohibited him from driving it, mandating that he travel instead by helicopter.

So just getting in an SUV or HUMVV to venture out onto Route Irish — all by itself — proclaimed that Haseltine was dead serious.

The tone of the conversation, where Haseltine asked the soldiers what they thought, instead of telling them what would solve their problem, was equally important. Many soldiers are used to being told what to do, instead of being first asked what they think is the right thing to do. The soldiers in the SUV that morning sensed that Haseltine, from his comment about DC not understanding what was happening downrange, actually did want to learn from them.

In other words, the soldiers had at least a small measure of respect for Haseltine and an equal sense they could trust him with the truth, up to a point, at least.

This trust and respect was all important to the truth coming out that morning. It did not arise because of Haseltine's rank, position, or mission, or anything formal at all, but because he actually seemed — to the soldiers — to care, at an emotional, human level, about keeping coalition soldiers from getting blown up.

Eavesdropping in the Green Zone communications center, Major Willis also probably picked up that caring tone in Haseltine's voice as he spoke with Greg back home, and was moved enough to approach the civilian.

Then, the back-and-forth ribbing and banter established that the two men "got each other" and shared a common purpose. Again, this all important, brief interaction led within minutes to a concrete next step solution to the Master Sergeant's challenge. It did not take place in a formal setting, but during a chance encounter with no power point slides, white papers or any other formalities so common in monster bureaucracies.

As with other chapters in this book, the actors are different, the story is different, the path to success different, but the underlying message is the same: innovation thrives in informal settings, especially when bonds of respect and trust emerge.

The lesson here is that monster bureaucracies can innovate with lightning speed if, through relationship building, you can persuade them to use weapons they already have in their arsenals in innovative new ways.

Conclusion:
The innovation equation

A simple way to boil down to one line everything we've said in this book is our version of an innovation equation:

$$\text{Innovation} = \frac{\text{Talent} + \text{Relationships}}{\text{Formality}}$$

where

- Talent represents the inventiveness and motivation of people involved

- Relationships represent the quantity and quality of emotional bonds those quality people have

- Formality represents the bureaucratic rigidness of the organization where those people work

Notice that formality, in this equation, doesn't merely subtract from innovation, it *divides* it in every sense of the word *divide*.

Why formality is so toxic to innovation

Candidly, our hope is that those of you who form the

backbone of the "rebel alliance" in your organization can take ideas from this book into C suites and boardrooms. The idea is not so much to get direct support for the innovations you cherish (because that's rarely realistic in next-quarter cultures), but to get some protection, if you will, from the antibodies in your organizations that are trying to kill you. Or, if the suits are unwilling or unable to tamp down corporate antibodies, at least to get the executives to leave you alone to toil in obscurity.

In other words, we want to help you prevent the monster bureaucracy from killing your innovation, because, left to its own, the monster likely *will* kill it.

Humans who have risen to C-suites and boardrooms like the ideas pitched to them to be simple and actionable (the higher level the executive, the simpler and more actionable the ideas need to be), so we came up with the innovation equation. It's simple and understandable with a quantitative flair because suits, who live and die by numbers, like things expressed in numbers.

The suits, if they are initially drawn to an idea, also want to know *why* the idea is the right idea in the first place.

So, here's how you can explain *why* formality is toxic, bearing in mind that the executives you are pitching got where they were by *faithfully serving the very formality you are challenging.*

Formality, in the form of written processes, procedures, organizational hierarchies, policies, and unwritten culture, exists in the first place for a very good reason: it codifies winning recipes for past successes to ensure continued success in the future. New hires need to know the best way to get things done, old hires need to be reminded, etc., etc. Thus, the goal of formality is to prevent deviations from proven recipes for success.

In other words, the goal of formality is to prevent change.

Thus, by definition, formality exists to kill innovation because innovation, especially game-changing innovation, represents big-time change.

This is all the suits need to hear on formality toxicity, because it's simple and pretty much says it all.

Why informality is so nurturing to innovation

The flip side of the formality coin — why informality is so healthy for innovation — takes a little more explaining and gets into the touchy-feely, squishy-soft, dare we say, *psychological* aspects of organizational behavior.

So tread carefully while trying to convince the suits to tolerate an easing of the iron grip they have spent their careers tightening. Perhaps discreetly remind them of tropes oft repeated in management books that good leaders manage tangibles while *great* leaders focus on intangibles. This trope isn't always true, by the way, but it will appeal to fantasies that most talented executives nurture deep in their hearts to be more visionary than reactionary.

The essence of the informality argument begins

with the *relationships* term in our innovation equation. It builds heavily on the concept of psychological safety, and its importance in the creative process so vital to all innovations.

We first learned of the term psychological safety while interviewing Sony Pictures Entertainment executive Nadya Ichinomiya for an article one of us was writing for Psychology Today. In a speech to the organization she chairs, Women in Technology, Hollywood, Nadya explained that psychological safety, defined by Harvard Professor Amy Edmonson, is *"The belief that one will not be punished or humiliated for speaking up with ideas, questions, concerns or mistakes."*

And when is it that people most believe they won't be punished or humiliated for bringing up radical ideas?

When they are with other people they trust, especially in informal settings like Chinese restaurants, where the goal of the interpersonal interaction isn't to advance an organization's agenda, but to sustain and strengthen emotional bonds among people.

So all-important psychological safety isn't something that organizations do; it's something that living, breathing *people* provide—or don't provide—to each other at an emotional level.

That's why fostering emotionally safe relationships is so vitally important to psychological safety, and in turn, creativity and innovation.

Another way to look at the importance of psychological safety is that psychological safety allows the human brain the luxury of wandering into uncharted waters in search of faster, better, cheaper ways of doing things, or doing things that have never been done before.

When we don't trust those around us, our brains, for very good reasons, spend all their energy on survival, constantly asking and answering questions such as: how do I avoid that landmine, stroke that ego, repeat this company mantra, or suck up to that fast-rising star without pissing off that fast-rising-star's powerful rival?

This sort of necessary internal dialogue, compelled by survival instincts, is antithetical to creativity, and creativity's close relative, innovation.

Thus, the informality of trusted personal relationship and psychological safety are inextricably intertwined, and both are incredibly important to fostering innovation.

All of this might suggest that leaders who want more innovation in their organizations should foster informal relationship building through company sports leagues, drama clubs, volunteer activities, free employee lunches where workers mingle and cross-pollinate, and other non-work-related social activities. And indeed, relaxed socializing among employees is a good thing that certainly won't hurt innovation.

But there's something inherently contradictory about the formal power structure of an organization consciously striving to foster the explicitly *informal*.

Thus, employees will inevitably sniff out what leadership is trying to do, and the informal gatherings will start to feel less like something employees want to do all on their own, and more like something *management wants* them to do, taking some of the sparkle and pizzazz out of the social activities.

Almost by definition, informal relationship building is a bottom-up, not top-down process, that must be allowed to develop naturally on its own. As such, the most that leaders can do is to acknowledge the awesome power of such bonding, then remove obstacles to bond-formation such as toxic employees that poison the workplace, turf-protecting bosses that discourage cross-department dialogue, or workspaces that make chance encounters rare among employees.

If, as a leader, you still feel compelled to do something proactive, then think of yourself as diligent gardener *after* the vegetable garden has already been planted in fertile soil: remove weeds, insects, snails, fungi, and other threats to your plants, water regularly, then let nature do the rest.

The talent term in the equation

None of what we've just said matters if talented, motivated people aren't at the heart of innovation efforts. No amount of easing-up of formal structures and strictures, no nurturing of informal relationships over chop suey will move the innovation ball down the field all by itself.

You have to have creative, out-of-the box thinkers, especially if you want revolutionary versus evolutionary advances.

But how do you find these people? What do you look for in a job interview?

That's a very deep question that could occupy an entire book (or two, or three) all by itself. Hints of a partial answer can be found by looking at the personality traits of innovators we have introduced in this book. For example, what traits did Crocker, Sojka, and Hibbeln all have in common?

To one degree or another, all of them were outsiders, who early in their lives felt isolated, and so later in their lives worked to forge human bonds that would ease their sense of isolation. And we assert that it was the formation of those strong bonds, even more than their necessary geniuses, that caused sparks to fly and to ignite revolutions.

We ran this idea by Leonard Kleinrock. You may recall him from Chapter 2 as the mind behind packet switching, the concept by which the internet runs today, and whose lab sent the very first message on the internet. He gave us this response.

Yes, so many of my colleagues from those golden days at MIT as a grad student, and in the early days of Arpanet/Internet, were "loners" or introverts, as you say. We were not the kind of kids/youth that followed the popular social modes of the day—we were, as I said, loners in so many ways. As an example, when I started building radios as a 6-7 year-old kid, I did not find pals to collaborate with; I did it alone, learning the hard way to overcome challenges. It never occurred to me to join a radio club or to become a HAM operator (heck, I couldn't afford the rig). Also, as you know, I couldn't afford to attend the no-tuition CCNY (I had to earn money for my family, working full time in the day in an industrial electronics firm in downtown Manhattan), so I went to night session there for 5-1/2 years to get my undergraduate EE degree—a totally lonely journey. The colleagues I can think of who manifested similar loner behavior are Larry Roberts, Ivan Sutherland, Claude Shannon, and more.

For readers who aren't part of the digital universe, Roberts, Sutherland, and Shannon weren't just stars, but mega-superstars who, along with Kleinrock, laid the foundations for the digital wonders we all enjoy today.

Thus, counter-intuitive as it seems, often the most productive relationship building—from the standpoint of innovation, at least—doesn't come from socially adept extroverts, but from more socially isolated introverts and "loners" seeking to fill emotional voids in their lives, and above all, to feel the psychological safety that is so vitally important to all of us, but especially those in "out groups."

So here, at last, we come to the bottom line of this book. Innovation isn't so much about processes, funding, or organization: it's all about talented people and their relationships, relationships that flourish because they are informal, and informal because informality nurtures trust — the most precious of all things that we, the social species called human, cherish.

Acknowledgements

We extend our deepest thanks to all those who were so generous with their time telling us their stories so that we could put them in the book.

We couldn't have written the book without many hours of participation of Brian Hibbeln, Gary Sojka, Stephen Crocker, and Mike Goslin, each of whom is featured in their own chapter.

At Disney, we wish to thank Bob Chapek, Arthur Bochner, Jackie Hart, and Allison Citino. Also, former Disney executives Kevin Mayer and Logan Olson, featured in the chapter "Harness Full Monster Power," were very helpful reviewing the manuscript. Thanks also to former Disney executive Marty Yudkovitz for the role he played at Disney in the events recounted here.

Our deepest gratitude goes to others who helped make this book a reality, including the Honorable Dutch Ruppersberger and his staff, Gwen Meyer, Steve Nixon, Jason Metheny, Vint Cerf, and Len Kleinrock.

We thank the Office of the Director of National Intelligence for promptly reviewing and approving the manuscript, and Laura and Joel Pitney and Jessica Hill at Launch My Book for editing and design of the book.

We are also grateful to Nadya Ichinomiya for her ideas and for calling our attention to the work of Amy Edmonson.

Finally, as most of the book focuses on technology innovation in national security, we extend our warmest gratitude towards the selfless women and men who serve our nation in the Military, Department of Defense, Intelligence Community, and other sectors of national security.

About the Authors

Eric Haseltine, PhD, is a named inventor on 58 patents, and former Executive Vice President of Walt Disney Imagineering. He served as Director of Research at NSA and Director of Science and Technology for the US Intelligence Community. Currently Chairman of the Board of the US Technology Leadership Council, he is author of 3 books on innovation, science and technology, including his recent espionage techno-thriller: *The Spy In Moscow Station*.

Chris Gilbert, MD, PhD, is a physician, writer, and speaker who has pioneered innovative techniques in holistic and integrative medicine, described in her recent book on mind-body medicine, *The Listening Cure*. Dr. Gilbert, who had private practices in France and California and served with Doctors Without Borders in Africa and Asia, is a certified specialist in Hyperbaric Medicine, and also regularly serves as medical consultant to TV and Motion Picture productions.

Made in the USA
Middletown, DE
13 July 2021

44034242R00078